CUPCAKE

Easy and Delicious Homemade Cupcake Recipes You Can Easily Make!

(The Best Vegan Cupcakes and Frostings)

Melinda Thomas

Published by Sharon Lohan

Cupcake Bakery: Easy and Delicious Homemade Cupcake Recipes You Can Easily Make! (The Best Vegan Cupcakes and Frostings)

ISBN 978-1-7776245-7-6

Legal & Disclaimer

The information contained in this book is not designed to replace or take the place of any form of medicine or professional medical advice. The information in this book has been provided for educational and entertainment purposes only.

Table of contents

PART 1

Introduction

What is a cupcake?

Honestly, if you don't know what a cupcake is, then you've probably been living under a rock for the past decade or so. For formality's sake though, let's try and define exactly what a cupcake is. A cupcake is exactly what it sounds like - they are cakes the size of small cups usually intended as single servings.

A lot of people enjoy making cupcakes just as much as eating them. This is mainly because of the fact that these delectable goodies are so flexible and easy to tweak. The number of cupcakes designs and recipes you can come up with is only limited to your imagination. All you need is a dash of innovation and a sprinkling of creativity!

Nevertheless, if you don't want to sweat about coming up with your own recipes, here are 31 of the tastiest and most popular recipes available on today's market. Feel free to use them to kick start your own imagination, impress your family and guests, or start your own small business!

Banana Cupcakes in Pastry Cream

Ingredients:
Banana cupcakes
- ½ tsp. salt
- 1 tsp. baking soda
- 1 ¼ tsp. baking powder
- 2 ¾ cups all-purpose flour
- ¼ cup vegetable shortening, softened
- ½ cup butter, unsalted, and softened
- 2 tsp. vanilla extract
- 1 ¾ cups sugar, granulated
- 2 whole eggs
- 1 ½ cups banana, ripe, and mashed
- ½ cup buttermilk
  Pastry cream
- 3 cups half-and-half
- ¼ tsp. salt
- 3 tbsp. cornstarch
- ½ cup sugar, granulated
- 6 egg yolks
- 1 tsp. vanilla extract

Procedure:
1. Preheat the oven to 325°F.
2. Use paper liners on 24 cupcake tins.
3. In a large bowl, combine the salt, baking soda, baking powder, and all-purpose flour.
4. Attach the paddle fitting to your electric mixer.
5. Place the shortening and butter in the mixing bowl.
6. Set the mixer on medium, and beat the butter for 3 minutes.
7. Once creamy, pour in the vanilla and sugar. Continue beating for 3 minutes.
8. Beat in the eggs. Make sure to scrape down the sides of the bowl occasionally.
9. Beat in the mashed bananas.
10. Once combined, set the mixer on low.
11. Gradually and alternately pour in the flour mixture and buttermilk. Remember to keep scraping the sides.
12. Once the batter has thoroughly combined, pour it into each lined cupcake tin. Make sure that the tins are only three-quarters full.
13. Bake for 25 minutes.
14. Remove from oven, and let cool for 20 minutes.
15. Remove the cupcakes from the tins, and place them on a wire rack.
16. While waiting for the cupcakes to cool completely, it's now time to make the pastry cream. To start, place a mesh sieve on a large bowl.
17. Set aside a piece of plastic wrap that is as big as the circumference of the large bowl.
18. Place a saucepan over a stove set on medium.
19. Heat the half-and-half in the saucepan. Once simmering, keep warm.
20. In a separate bowl, combine the salt, cornstarch, sugar, and egg yolks.
21. Once the mixture turns pale, whisk in the heated 1 ½ cups half-and-half.

22. Pour this egg mixture back into the pan.
23. Cook while stirring constantly for around 6 minutes.
24. Remove the pan from heat, and stir in the vanilla.
25. Strain this mixture through the mesh sieve.
26. Place the prepared plastic wrap directly on the cream.
27. Refrigerate the bowl.
28. After one hour, both the cream and cupcakes should have considerably cooled.
29. Using either a spatula or pastry bag, top the cupcakes with the pastry cream.
30. Garnish with a dried banana chip, if preferred.
31. Best served chilled!

Dark Chocolate Cupcakes with Peanut Butter Topping

Ingredients:

Dark chocolate cupcakes

- ½ cup cocoa powder, Dutch-processed
- ¾ cup chocolate, bittersweet, and chopped
- 8 tbsp. butter, unsalted, and softened
- ¾ tsp. baking powder
- ½ tsp. baking soda

- ¾ cup all-purpose flour
- 2 whole eggs
- ½ tsp. salt
- 1 tsp. vanilla extract
- ¾ cup sugar, granulated
- ½ cup sour cream
  Peanut butter topping
- ¼ tsp. salt
- ¾ tsp. vanilla extract
- 5 tbsp. butter, unsalted, and softened
- 1 cup peanut butter, creamy
- 1 cup sugar, confectioners'
- 1/3 cup heavy cream

Procedure:
1. Preheat the oven to 350°F.
2. Place the rack in the lower-middle.
3. Use paper liners on 12 cupcake tins.
4. Pour a few cups of water into a saucepan.
5. Stir together the cocoa, chocolate, and butter in a medium bowl.
6. Place the bowl in the saucepan.
7. Place the pan over a stove set on medium.
8. Once the chocolate and butter melt, whisk them together to combine. Set aside to cool.
9. In a small bowl, mix the baking powder, baking soda, and all-purpose flour. Set aside.
10. In a separate bowl, beat the eggs together.
11. Whisk in the salt, vanilla, and sugar.
12. Once fluffy, whisk in the butter mixture.
13. Whisk in the sour cream.
14. Gradually whisk in the flour mixture until the batter thickens.
15. Pour the batter into the lined cupcake tins.
16. Bake for 20 minutes.
17. Remove from oven, and let cool for 15 minutes.

18. Remove the cupcakes from the tins, and place them on a wire rack for half an hour.
19. While waiting, pour all of the peanut butter topping ingredients, except for the heavy cream, into a mixing bowl.
20. Attach the paddle fitting to your electric mixer.
21. Set the mixer on medium-low. Remember to keep scraping the sides of the bowl.
22. Set the mixer on high, and beat in the heavy cream.
23. Once the topping smooth, turn off the mixer.
24. Using either a spatula or pastry bag, top the cupcakes with the pastry cream.
25. Serve.

Irish Car Bombs

Ingredients:
Cupcakes
- 1 cup butter, unsalted, and softened
- 1 cup Guinness stout
- ¾ cup cocoa powder, Dutch-processed
- ¾ tsp. salt
- 1 ½ tsp. baking soda
- 2 cups sugar, granulated
- 2 cups all-purpose flour
- 2/3 cup sour cream
- 2 whole eggs

Whiskey ganache
- 8 oz. chocolate, bittersweet, and chopped
- 2/3 cup heavy cream
- 2 tsp. Irish whiskey
- 2 tbsp. butter, softened

Baileys topping
- 2 cups butter, unsalted, and softened
- 5 cups sugar, powdered
- 6 tbsp. Baileys Irish Cream

Procedure:
1. Preheat the oven to 350°F.
2. Use paper liners on 24 cupcake tins.
3. Stir together the butter and Guinness in a saucepan.
4. Place the pan over a stove set on medium.
5. Whisk in the cocoa until smooth.
6. Remove the pan from the heat, and set aside to cool.
7. In a large bowl, combine the salt, baking soda, sugar, and all-purpose flour. Set aside.
8. Using an electric mixer set on medium, beat together the sour cream and eggs.
9. Beat in the chocolate mixture.
10. Set the mixture on low, and gradually beat in the flour. Remember to occasionally scrape the sides of the bowl.
11. Once the batter has thoroughly combined, pour it into each lined cupcake tin. Make sure that the tins are only three-quarters full.
12. Bake for 17 minutes.
13. Remove from oven, and let cool for 20 minutes.
14. Remove the cupcakes from the tins, and place them on a wire rack.
15. While waiting, make the whiskey ganache. To start, place the chocolate bits into a bowl.
16. Pour the heavy cream into a saucepan.

17. Place the pan over a stove set on medium.
18. Once the cream begins to simmer, pour it into the bowl of chocolate. Stir to combine using a spatula.
19. Pour in the remaining ganache ingredients. Stir until smooth.
20. Set aside to cool and thicken slightly.
21. While waiting, use a small cookie cutter to remove the center of each cupcake. Make sure the hole is around two-thirds of the cupcake in depth.
22. Pipe the ganache into each cupcake center until full. Set aside.
23. Attach the whisk fitting to your electric mixer.
24. Place the butter in the mixing bowl.
25. Set the mixer on medium-high, and whisk the butter for 5 minutes. Remember to occasionally scrape the sides of the bowl.
26. Set the mixer on medium-low, and gradually whisk in all the sugar.
27. Set the mixer on medium-high, and whisk in the Irish cream for 3 minutes or until fluffy.
28. Using either a spatula or pastry bag, top the cupcakes with the pastry cream.
29. Use sprinkles for decoration.

Lemon-Limoncello Cupcakes

Ingredients:
Cupcakes
- ½ tsp. salt
- 1 tsp. baking powder
- 1 ½ cups all-purpose flour
- 1 cup sugar, granulated
- 2 oz. cream cheese, softened
- 2 oz. butter, unsalted, and softened
- 3 whole eggs
- 2 tbsp. limoncello
- ½ cup buttermilk
- 1 lemon, zested
- ¼ cup lemon juice
  Lemon curd
- ¼ cup sugar, granulated
- ½ cup lemon juice
- 2 lemons, zested
- 1 whole egg
- 1 egg yolk
  Limoncello frosting
- 4 oz. cream cheese, softened

- 2 oz. butter, unsalted, and softened
- 1 tbsp. limoncello
- 2 cups sugar, powdered, and sifted

Procedure:

1. Preheat the oven to 350°F.
2. Use paper liners on 12 cupcake tins.
3. Place the rack in the middle of the oven.
4. In a large bowl, sift together the salt, baking powder, and flour. Set aside.
5. Attach the paddle fitting to your electric mixer.
6. Set the mixer on medium, and beat together the sugar, cream cheese, and butter.
7. Once the mixture is creamy, beat the eggs in one at a time.
8. Beat in the limocello for 1 minute.
9. Set the mixer on low, and alternately beat in the flour mixture and buttermilk.
10. Beat in the lemon zest and juice.
11. Once the batter has thoroughly combined, pour it into each lined cupcake tin. Make sure that the tins are only three-quarters full.
12. Bake for 20 minutes.
13. Remove from oven, and let cool for 20 minutes.
14. Remove the cupcakes from the tins, and place them on a wire rack.
15. While waiting for the cupcakes to cool, it's time to make the lemon curd. To start, place a saucepan over a stove set on medium.
16. Stir in the sugar, lemon zest, and juice. Let simmer for a few minutes.
17. In a separate bowl, beat the whole egg together with the egg yolk.
18. Whisk in the heated lemon mixture into the bowl of eggs.
19. Once the eggs are tempered, pour the mixture back into the pan.

20. Cook the mixture over medium heat for 5 minutes. Stir constantly.
21. Remove the pan from the heat. Set aside to cool.
22. While waiting for the lemon curd to cool, make the limocello frosting. To start, place the cream cheese and butter in a mixing bowl.
23. Set the mixer on medium, and beat the ingredients together for 3 minutes.
24. Beat in the limocello for 1 minute.
25. Set the mixture on low, and gradually beat in the sugar until smooth.
26. Use a small cookie cutter to remove the center of each cupcake. Make sure the hole is around two-thirds of the cupcake in depth.
27. Pipe the lemon curd into each cupcake center until full.
28. Using either a spatula or pastry bag, top the cupcakes with the limoncello frosting.
29. Garnish with berries and lemon slices.

Margarita Cupcakes

Ingredients:
Cupcakes

- ¼ tsp. salt
- 1½ tsp. baking powder
- 1½ cups all-purpose flour
- 1 cup sugar, granulated
- ½ cup butter, unsalted, and softened
- 2 whole eggs
- 2 tbsp. tequila
- ¼ tsp. vanilla extract
- 1 ½ limes, zested, and juiced
- ½ cup buttermilk
- 2 tbsp. tequila, to brush
  Tequila Frosting
- 1 cup butter, unsalted, and softened
- 2¾ cups sugar, powdered
- ½ tsp. table salt
- 2 tbsp. tequila
- 1 tbsp. lime juice
  Procedure:
1. Preheat the oven to 350°F.
2. Use paper liners on 12 cupcake tins.
3. In a large bowl, sift together the salt, baking powder, and flour. Set aside.
4. Attach the paddle fitting to your electric mixer.
5. Set the mixer on medium, and beat together the sugar and butter.
6. Once the mixture is creamy, beat the eggs in one at a time. Remember to occasionally scrape the sides of the bowl.
7. Beat in the tequila, vanilla extract, lime juice, and zest.
8. Set the mixer on low, and alternately beat in the flour mixture and buttermilk.
9. Once the batter has thoroughly combined, pour it into each lined cupcake tin. Make sure that the tins are only three-quarters full.
10. Bake for 25 minutes.
11. Remove from oven, and let cool for 10 minutes.

12. Remove the cupcakes from the tins, brush them with 2 tbsp. of tequila, and place them on a wire rack to cool completely.
13. While waiting for the cupcakes to cool, it's time to make the tequila frosting. To start, attach the whisk fitting to the electric mixer.
14. Place the butter in a mixing bowl.
15. Whisk the butter on medium-high for 5 minutes.
16. Set the mixer on medium-low, and whisk in the sugar gradually. Remember occasionally to scrape the sides of the bowl.
17. Set the mixer on medium-high, and pour in the salt, tequila, and lime juice.
18. Once the frosting is fluffy, turn off the mixer.
19. Using either a spatula or pastry bag, top the cupcakes with the limoncello frosting.
20. Garnish with lime zest and salt, if desired.

Mocha Cupcakes in Espresso Frosting

Ingredients:
Mocha cupcakes
- 1 ½ tsp. espresso powder
- ½ cup brewed coffee, extra-strong
- 1 tsp. vanilla extract

- ½ cup whole milk
- ¼ tsp. salt
- ½ tsp. baking soda
- 1 tsp. baking powder
- 1/3 cup cocoa powder, unsweetened
- 1 1/3 cups all-purpose flour
- ½ cup sugar, brown
- ½ cup sugar, granulated
- ½ cup butter, unsalted, and softened
- 1 whole egg
  Espresso frosting
- 1 ½ tsp. espresso powder
- 1 ½ tsp. vanilla extract
- 1 cup butter, unsalted, and softened
- 2 ½ cups sugar, powdered

Procedure:
1. Preheat the oven to 350°F.
2. Use paper liners on 12 cupcake tins.
3. Stir the espresso into the coffee. Let cool completely.
4. Stir in the vanilla, and milk. Set aside.
5. Sift together the salt, baking soda, baking powder, cocoa, and all-purpose flour in a bowl.
6. Attach the whisk fitting to your electric mixer.
7. Place the sugars and butter in a mixing bowl.
8. Set the mixer on medium-high, and whisk the butter mixture together for 3 minutes.
9. Once the mixture is fluffy, beat in the egg.
10. Set the mixer on low, and alternately beat in the flour and coffee mixtures.
11. Once the batter has thoroughly combined, pour it into each lined cupcake tin. Make sure that the tins are only three-quarters full.
12. Bake for 20 minutes.

13. Remove from oven, and let cool for 10 minutes.
14. Remove the cupcakes from the tins, and place them on a wire rack to cool completely.
15. While waiting for cupcakes to cool, it's time to make the espresso frosting. To start, stir the espresso into the vanilla. Set aside.
16. Place the butter in a mixing bowl.
17. Set the mixer on medium-high, and whisk the butter for 5 minutes.
18. Set the mixer on low, and gradually whisk in the sugar. Remember to keep scraping the sides of the mixing bowl.
19. Once the last of the sugar has been added, set the mixer on medium-high and let whisk for another 2 minutes.
20. Stir in the prepared vanilla mixture.
21. Once the frosting is fluffy, turn off the mixer.
22. Using either a spatula or pastry bag, top the cupcakes with the espresso frosting.
23. Enjoy!

Pumpkin Cupcakes in Cream Cheese Frosting

Ingredients:
Pumpkin cupcakes

10. Once the batter has thoroughly combined, pour it into each lined cupcake tin. Make sure that the tins are only three-quarters full.
11. Bake for 18 minutes.
12. Remove from oven, and let cool for 10 minutes.
13. Remove the cupcakes from the tins, and place them on a wire rack to cool completely.
14. While waiting for the cupcakes to cool, it's time to make the cream cheese frosting. To start, place the cream cheese and butter in a mixing bowl.
15. Set the mixer on medium-high, and beat the ingredients together for 3 minutes.
16. Once the mixture turn fluffy, set the mixer on low.
17. Gradually beat in the sugar, followed by the vanilla.
18. Once the frosting is fluffy, turn off the mixer.
19. Using either a spatula or pastry bag, top the cupcakes with the cream cheese frosting.
20. Serve chilled, if preferred.

Red Velvet Cupcakes in

- ¼ tsp. cloves, ground
- 1 tsp. nutmeg, grated
- 2 tsp. cinnamon, ground
- 1 tbsp. ginger, ground
- 1 tsp. salt
- 1 tbsp. plus 1 tsp. baking powder
- 1 tsp. baking soda
- 4 cups cake flour, sifted
- 2 ½ cups sugar, brown
- 1 cup butter, unsalted, and softened
- 4 whole eggs
- 1 cup butter milk
- 1 ½ cups pumpkin, canned

Cream cheese frosting

- 12 oz. cream cheese, softened
- 1 cup butter, unsalted, and softened
- 4 cups sugar, confectioners'
- ¾ tsp. vanilla extract

- ¼ tsp. cloves, ground
- 1 tsp. nutmeg, grated
- 2 tsp. cinnamon, ground
- 1 tbsp. ginger, ground
- 1 tsp. salt
- 1 tbsp. plus 1 tsp. baking powder
- 1 tsp. baking soda
- 4 cups cake flour, sifted
- 2 ½ cups sugar, brown
- 1 cup butter, unsalted, and softened
- 4 whole eggs
- 1 cup butter milk
- 1 ½ cups pumpkin, canned
  Cream cheese frosting
- 12 oz. cream cheese, softened
- 1 cup butter, unsalted, and softened
- 4 cups sugar, confectioners'
- ¾ tsp. vanilla extract

Procedure:
1. Preheat the oven to 350°F.
2. Use paper liners on 32 cupcake tins.
3. Combine the spices, salt, baking powder, baking soda, and cake flour. Set aside.
4. Attach the paddle fitting on the electric mixer.
5. Place the sugar and butter in a mixing bowl.
6. Set the mixer on medium-high, and mix both ingredients until fluffy.
7. Gradually beat in the eggs. Remember to occasionally scrape the sides of the bowl.
8. Set the mixer on low, and alternately beat in the flour mixture and buttermilk.
9. Once the mixture is smooth, beat in the canned pumpkin.

10. Once the batter has thoroughly combined, pour it into each lined cupcake tin. Make sure that the tins are only three-quarters full.
11. Bake for 18 minutes.
12. Remove from oven, and let cool for 10 minutes.
13. Remove the cupcakes from the tins, and place them on a wire rack to cool completely.
14. While waiting for the cupcakes to cool, it's time to make the cream cheese frosting. To start, place the cream cheese and butter in a mixing bowl.
15. Set the mixer on medium-high, and beat the ingredients together for 3 minutes.
16. Once the mixture turn fluffy, set the mixer on low.
17. Gradually beat in the sugar, followed by the vanilla.
18. Once the frosting is fluffy, turn off the mixer.
19. Using either a spatula or pastry bag, top the cupcakes with the cream cheese frosting.
20. Serve chilled, if preferred.

Red Velvet Cupcakes in Cream Cheese Topping

Ingredients:
Red velvet cupcakes

18

- 3 tbsp. food coloring, red
- ½ tsp. vanilla extract
- 2 ½ tbsp. cocoa powder, unsweetened
- ¾ cup sugar, granulated
- 4 tbsp. butter, unsalted, and softened
- 1 whole egg
- ½ cup buttermilk
- 1 cup plus 2 tbsp. all-purpose flour
- 1 ½ tsp. white vinegar, distilled
- ½ tsp. baking soda
- ½ tsp. salt
  Cream cheese topping
- ½ tsp. salt
- 4 oz. cream cheese, softened
- 4 oz. butter, unsalted, and softened
- 2 ½ cups sugar, powdered
- 1 tbsp. vanilla extract
  Procedure:
1. Preheat the oven to 350°F.
2. Use paper liners on 12 cupcake tins.
3. In a small bowl, stir together the food coloring, vanilla, and cocoa. Set aside.
4. Attach the whisk fitting to the electric mixer.
5. Place the sugar and butter in a mixing bowl.
6. Set the mixer on medium-high, and whisk the butter mixture for 3 minutes.
7. Once the mixture is fluffy, set the mixer on high, and whisk in the egg. Remember to occasionally scrape the sides of the bowl.
8. Set the mixer on medium, and whisk in the prepared cocoa mixture until well combined.
9. Once the batter is evenly colored, set the mixer on low, and whisk in half of the buttermilk followed by half of the flour. Scrape down the sides of the bowl, and repeat with the other half.

10. Set the mixer on high, and continue whisking for another two minutes.
11. Set the mixer on low, and whisk in the vinegar, baking soda, and salt.
12. Set the mixer on high, and continue whisking for another two minutes.
13. Once the batter has thoroughly combined, pour it into each lined cupcake tin. Make sure that the tins are only three-quarters full.
14. Bake for 20 minutes.
15. Remove from oven, and let cool for 10 minutes.
16. Remove the cupcakes from the tins, and place them on a wire rack to cool completely.
17. While waiting for the cupcakes to cool, it's time to make the cream cheese frosting. To start, place the salt, cream cheese, and butter in a mixing bowl.
18. Set the mixer on high, and whisk the ingredients together for 5 minutes.
19. Set the mixer on low, and gradually whisk in the sugar.
20. Whisk in the vanilla, and set the mixer on medium-high.
21. Once the frosting is fluffy, turn off the mixer.
22. Using either a spatula or pastry bag, top the cupcakes with the cream cheese frosting.
23. Enjoy!

Tiramisu Cupcakes

Ingredients:
Cupcakes
- ½ tsp. salt
- ¾ baking powder
- 1 ¼ cups cake flour, sifted
- ¼ cup milk
- 1 vanilla bean, halved, and seeds reserved
- 4 tbsp. butter, unsalted, softened, and chopped
- 1 cup sugar, granulated
- 3 whole eggs
- 3 egg yolks
  Espresso syrup
- ¼ cup sugar, granulated
- 1 oz. marsala
- 1/3 cup plus 1 tbsp. espresso
  Mascarpone topping
- 1 cup heavy cream
- ½ cup sugar, confectioners'
- 8 oz. mascarpone cheese, softened
- Cocoa powder for dusting
  Procedure:
1. Preheat the oven to 325°F.
2. Use paper liners on 18 cupcake tins.

3. In a large bowl, combine the salt, baking powder, and flour. Set aside.
4. Pour the milk into a small saucepan.
5. Stir in the vanilla pod and seeds.
6. Place the pan over a stove set on medium.
7. Heat the mixture while stirring.
8. Once bubbles start to form, remove the pan from the heat.
9. Stir in the butter, and let the mixture stand for around 15 minutes.
10. Place a fine sieve over a small bowl.
11. Strain the butter mixture through the sieve. Discard the vanilla pod. Set aside.
12. Attach the whisk fitting to the electric mixer.
13. Place the sugar, whole eggs, and yolks in a mixing bowl.
14. Heat a pan full of water until it begins to simmer.
15. Place the bowl of eggs in the water.
16. Whisk the ingredients together for 6 minutes.
17. Remove the mixture from the heat.
18. Set the electric mixer to high, and whisk the mixture until fluffy.
19. In three batches, fold the prepared flour mixture into the egg mixture.
20. Scoop out ½ cup of the batter, and stir it into the prepared milk mixture.
21. Fold the resulting milk mixture into the bowl of remaining batter.
22. Once the batter has thoroughly combined, pour it into each lined cupcake tin. Make sure that the tins are only three-quarters full.
23. Bake for 20 minutes.
24. Remove from oven, and let cool for 10 minutes.
25. Remove the cupcakes from the tins, and place them on a wire rack to cool completely.

26. While waiting for the cupcakes to cool, it's time to make the syrup. To start, stir together the sugar, marsala, and espresso. Let stand to cool.
27. Brush the resulting syrup on the cooled cupcakes. Let stand for half an hour.
28. While waiting for the cupcakes to absorb the syrup, make the mascarpone topping. To begin, place the heavy cream into a mixing bowl.
29. Set the mixer on medium, and beat the cream until a little stiff. Be careful not to overbeat. This will cause the topping to be grainy.
30. In a separate bowl, combine the sugar and marscapone.
31. Fold the sugar mixture into the cream.
32. Using either a spatula or pastry bag, top the cupcakes with the resulting mixture.
33. Use cocoa powder to dust before serving.

Vanilla Cupcakes in Butter Cream Frosting

Ingredients:
Cupcakes
- ½ tsp. salt
- 1 ½ tsp. baking powder
- 1 cup sugar, granulated
- 1 ½ cups all-purpose flour

- 1 ½ tsp. vanilla extract
- 1 whole egg
- 1 egg yolk
- ½ cup sour cream
- 8 oz. butter, unsalted, and softened
  Butter cream frosting
- 1 cup butter, unsalted, and softened
- 2 ½ cups sugar, powdered
- 1 tbsp. vanilla extract

Procedure:
1. Preheat the oven to 350°F.
2. Use paper liners on 12 cupcake tins.
3. In a large bowl, combine the salt, baking powder, sugar, and flour. Set aside.
4. Attach the paddle fitting to the electric mixer.
5. Place the vanilla, whole egg, yolk, sour cream, and butter in a mixing bowl.
6. Set the mixer on medium, and beat the mixture together for 30 seconds.
7. Set the mixer on low, and beat in the prepared flour mixture. Remember to occasionally scrape the sides of the bowl.
8. Once the batter has thoroughly combined, pour it into each lined cupcake tin. Make sure that the tins are only three-quarters full.
9. Bake for 24 minutes.
10. Remove from oven, and let cool for 10 minutes.
11. Remove the cupcakes from the tins, and place them on a wire rack to cool completely.
12. While waiting for the cupcakes to cool, it's time to make the frosting. To start, attach the whisk fitting to the electric mixer.
13. Place the butter in a mixing bowl.

14. Set the mixer on medium-high, and whisk the butter for 5 minutes.
15. Set the mixer on low, and gradually whisk in the sugar.
16. Set the mixer on medium-high, and whisk in the vanilla for 2 minutes.
17. Once the frosting is fluffy, turn off the mixer.
18. Using either a spatula or pastry bag, top the cupcakes with the butter cream frosting.
19.   Serve.

Chocolate Whiskey and Beer Cupcakes

Ingredients:
Cupcakes
- 1 cup butter, unsalted, and softened
- 1 cup stout
- ¾ cup cocoa powder, unsweetened
- ¾ tsp. salt
- 1 ½ tsp. baking soda
- 2 cups sugar
- 2 cups all-purpose flour
- 2/3 cup sour cream
- 2 whole eggs
  Ganache filling

- 8 oz. chocolate, bittersweet, and chopped
- 2/3 cup heavy cream
- 2 tbsp. Irish whiskey
- 2 tbsp. butter, softened
  Bailey's frosting
- 4 cups sugar, confectioners'
- 4 oz. butter, unsalted, and softened
- 4 tbsp. Baileys Irish Cream

Procedure:
1. Preheat the oven to 350°F.
2. Use paper liners on 24 cupcake tins.
3. Place a saucepan over a stove set on medium.
4. While simmering, whisk together the butter and stout in the pan.
5. Whisk in the cocoa until smooth. Set aside to cool.
6. In a large bowl, combine the salt, baking soda, sugar, and flour. Set aside.
7. Attach the whisk fitting to the electric mixer.
8. Place the sour cream and eggs in a mixing bowl.
9. Set the mixer on medium, and whisk the mixture together until well combined.
10. Whisk in the stout mixture.
11. Set the mixer on low, and gradually whisk in the flour mixture.
12. Once the batter has thoroughly combined, pour it into each lined cupcake tin. Make sure that the tins are only three-quarters full.
13. Bake for 17 minutes.
14. Remove from oven, and let cool for 10 minutes.
15. Remove the cupcakes from the tins, and place them on a wire rack to cool completely.
16. While waiting for the cupcakes to cool, it's time to make the ganache. To start, place the chocolate in a bowl.

17. Pour the cream into a saucepan.
18. Place the pan over a stove set on medium, and heat until simmering.
19. Pour the heated cream over the chocolate. Let sit for 1 minute.
20. Whisk the mixture together until thoroughly combined.
21. Whisk in the whiskey and butter. Let cool for a few minutes.
22. While waiting, use a small cookie cutter to remove the center of each cupcake. Make sure the hole is around two-thirds of the cupcake in depth.
23. Pipe the ganache into each cupcake center until full. Set aside.
24. Attach the whisk fitting to your electric mixer.
25. Place the butter in the mixing bowl.
26. Set the mixer on medium-high, and whisk the butter for 5 minutes. Remember to occasionally scrape the sides of the bowl.
27. Set the mixer on medium-low, and gradually whisk in all the sugar.
28. Set the mixer on medium-high, and whisk in the Irish cream for 3 minutes or until fluffy.
29. Using either a spatula or pastry bag, top the cupcakes with the frosting.
30. Use sprinkles for decoration.

Snow-topped Holiday Cupcakes

Ingredients:
Coconut cupcakes
- ¾ tsp. nutmeg
- ¾ tsp. salt
- ½ tsp. baking soda
- 2 ½ cups plus 2 tbsp. all-purpose flour, bleached, and unsifted
- 12 tbsp. butter, unsalted, and softened
- 1 ½ cups sugar, confectioners'
- 3 whole eggs
- 2 ½ tsp. vanilla extract
- ¾ cup sour cream
- 1 cup coconut flakes, sweetened
Coconut cream frosting
- 5 tbsp. butter, unsalted, and softened
- 12 oz. cream cheese, softened
- 1/8 tsp. nutmeg, grated
- 3 tbsp. heavy cream
- 2 ½ tsp. vanilla extract
- ¾ cup coconut flakes, sweetened
- 5 ½ cups sugar, confectioners'
Topping
- 1 ½ cups coconut flakes, sweetened

Procedure:
1. Preheat the oven to 350°F.
2. Use paper liners on 8 jumbo cupcake tins.
3. In a sheet of wax paper, combine the nutmeg, salt, baking soda, and flour. Set aside.
4. Place the butter in a mixing bowl.
5. Set the mixer to medium, and beat the butter for 3 minutes.
6. Beat in half of the sugar for 2 minutes. Repeat with the remaining half.
7. Pour in the eggs one at a time.
8. Beat in the vanilla. Remember to occasionally scrape the sides of the bowl.
9. Set the mixer on low, and alternately beat in the flour mixture and sour cream.
10. Once smooth, beat in the coconut flakes.
11. Pour the resulting batter into each lined cupcake tin. Make sure that the tins are only three-quarters full.
12. Bake for half an hour.
13. Remove from oven, and let cool for 15 minutes.
14. Remove the cupcakes from the tins, and place them on a wire rack to cool completely.
15. While waiting for the cupcakes to cool, it's time to make the frosting. To start, place the butter and cream cheese in a mixing bowl.
16. Set the mixer on medium, and beat together for a minute.
17. Beat in the nutmeg, heavy cream, and vanilla.
18. Set the mixer on low, and gradually beat in the coconut flakes and sugar.
19. Once the frosting is fluffy, turn off the mixer.
20. Use a spatula or pastry bag to top the cupcakes with the cream cheese.
21. Sprinkle coconut flakes over the frosting.

Strawberry Cupcakes

Ingredients:
- 12 oz. strawberries, fresh, rinsed, stems removed, and chopped
- 2 tbsp. sugar, caster
- 1 cup butter, unsalted, and softened
- 1 ¼ cup sugar, granulated
- 4 whole eggs
- ¼ tsp. almond extract
- 1 tsp. vanilla extract
- 2 ½ tsp. baking powder
- ¼ tsp. salt
- 2 ¾ cups cake flour, sifted
- ½ cup whole milk

Procedure:
1. Place the strawberries into a bowl.
2. Pour in a few tbsp. of water.
3. Stir in the sugar to coat.
4. Refrigerate overnight.
5. Mash the bowl of strawberries using a fork.
6. Place a mesh sieve over a bowl.
7. Juice the strawberries through the sieve. Reserve the juice.
8. Preheat the oven to 350°F.

9. Use paper liners on 12 cupcake tins.
10. Place the butter and sugar in a mixing bowl.
11. Set the mixer on medium, and beat the butter mixture for 3 minutes.
12. Set the mixer on medium-low, and beat in the eggs one at a time. Remember to occasionally scrape the sides of the bowl.
13. Beat in the almond and vanilla extract for 30 seconds.
14. In a separate bowl, combine the baking powder, salt, and flour.
15. Set the mixer on low, and alternately beat in the milk and flour.
16. Beat in strawberries and ¼ cup of the strawberry juice.
17. Once the batter has thoroughly combined, pour it into each lined cupcake tin. Make sure that the tins are only three-quarters full.
18. Bake for 22 minutes.
19. Remove from oven, and let cool for 10 minutes.
20. Remove the cupcakes from the tins, and place them on a wire rack to cool completely.
21. Brush the surface of the cupcakes with the remaining strawberry juice.
22. Frost decoratively, if desired.

Chocolate Cupcakes with Brandied Berries and Chantilly Cream

Ingredients:
Brandied berries
- 1 lb. strawberries, fresh, rinsed, hulled, and diced finely
- ¼ cup honey
- 1 cup brandy
Chocolate cupcakes
- ½ tsp. salt
- 1 tsp. baking soda
- 1 tsp. baking powder
- ½ cup cocoa powder
- 2 cups sugar
- 1 ¾ cups all-purpose flour
- 2 whole eggs
- 1 cup milk
- ½ cup canola oil
- 1 cup brewed coffee
Chantilly cream
- 1 pint whipping cream
- 1 tsp. vanilla
- 2 tbsp. sugar

Procedure:
1. Preheat the oven to 350°F.
2. In a large bowl, stir together the honey and brandy.
3. Marinate the strawberries in the mixture for an hour.
4. Use paper liners on 12 cupcake tins.
5. In a large bowl, sift together the salt, baking soda, baking powder, cocoa, sugar, and flour. Set aside.
6. Whisk in the eggs one at a time, followed by the oil, and then the coffee.
7. Once the batter has thoroughly combined, pour it into each lined cupcake tin. Make sure that the tins are only three-quarters full.
8. Bake for 20 minutes.
9. Remove from oven, and let cool for 10 minutes.
10. Remove the cupcakes from the tins, and place them on a wire rack to cool completely.
11. Using an electric mixer, whisk the cream until it forms peaks.
12. Whisk in the vanilla and sugar. Be careful not to overbeat. Set aside.
13. Use a small cookie cutter to remove the center of each cupcake. Make sure the hole is around two-thirds of the cupcake in depth.
14. Pipe the brandied strawberries into each cupcake center until full.
15. Frost with the prepared cream.
16. Sprinkle with some grated chocolate, and garnish with sliced strawberries.

Raspberry Lemon Cupcakes

Ingredients:
Cupcakes
- 2 ¼ cups cake flour
- 1 tbsp. baking powder
- ½ tsp. salt
- 1 ¼ cups buttermilk
- 4 egg whites
- 1 ½ cups sugar
- 2 lemons, zested
- 8 tbsp. butter, unsalted, and softened
- 1 tsp. vanilla extract
- ½ tsp. lemon extract
  Raspberry butter cream
- 1 stick butter, salted, and softened
- 1 stick butter, unsalted, and softened
- ½ cup shortening
- 1 tbsp. vanilla extract
- ½ tsp. raspberry extract
- ½ cup raspberries, pureed
- 1 ½ lbs. sugar, confectioners'
- 4 tbsp. milk, very cold

Procedure:

1. Preheat the oven to 350°F.
2. Use paper liners on 12 cupcake tins.
3. In a large bowl, combine the salt, baking powder, and flour. Set aside.
4. In a separate bowl, stir together the egg whites and milk. Set aside.
5. Attach the paddle fitting to the electric mixer.
6. Use your hands to rub the sugar and lemon zest together in a mixing bowl.
7. Add the butter to the bowl.
8. Set the mixer on medium, and beat the mixture for 3 minutes.
9. Beat in the lemon and vanilla extract.
10. Set the mixer on low, and beat in a third of the flour mixture followed by half of the milk mixture. Repeat until you use up both mixtures.
11. Set the mixer on medium, and continue beating for another 2 minutes.
12. Once the batter has thoroughly combined, pour it into each lined cupcake tin. Make sure that the tins are only three-quarters full.
13. Bake for 20 minutes.
14. Remove from oven, and let cool for 10 minutes.
15. Remove the cupcakes from the tins, and place them on a wire rack to cool completely.
16. While waiting for the cupcakes to cool, make the butter cream. To start, place the shortening and butter in a mixing bowl.
17. Set the mixer on medium, and beat the ingredients together until thoroughly combined.
18. Beat in the raspberry and vanilla extract.
19. Beat in the raspberry puree.
20. Set the mixer on low, and gradually beat in the sugar.

21. Continue beating while adding just enough cold milk to achieve the desired consistency.
22. Use the butter cream to frost the cooled cupcakes.
23. Try chilled.

Peaches and Cream Cupcakes

Ingredients:
Cupcakes
- 5 oz. butter, softened
- 5 oz. sugar,
- 3 whole eggs
- 2 tsp. vanilla extract
- 5 oz. all-purpose flour
- 2 tsp. baking powder
- 2 peaches, ripe, and diced
  Cream topping
- 2 tbsp. cream cheese
- 3 tbsp. sugar, confectioners'
- Peach syrup to taste

Procedure:
1. Preheat the oven to 350°F.
2. Use paper liners on 12 cupcake tins.

3. Attach the paddle fitting to the electric mixer.
4. Place the sugar and butter in a mixing bowl.
5. Set the mixer on medium, and beat the mixture until fluffy.
6. Beat in one of the eggs.
7. Beat in the vanilla extract and half the baking powder, followed by half the flour.
8. Beat in the rest of the eggs, and the remaining baking powder and flour. Remember to occasionally scrape the sides of the bowl.
9. Once the batter has thoroughly combined, pour it into each lined cupcake tin. Make sure that the tins are only three-quarters full.
10. Bake for 25 minutes.
11. Remove from oven, and let cool for 10 minutes.
12. Remove the cupcakes from the tins, and place them on a wire rack to cool completely.
13. While waiting for the cupcakes to cool, make the cream topping. To do this, simply whisk together the three ingredients in a small bowl.
14. Frost the cooled cupcakes with the prepared topping.
15. Garnish with peach slices, if desired.

Cardamom Cupcakes in Cream Cheese Frosting

Ingredients:
Cardamom cupcakes
- ¼ tsp. salt
- ¼ tsp. baking soda
- 1 tsp. baking powder
- ¼ tsp. cinnamon
- ½ tsp. cardamom
- ¾ cup sugar
- 1/3 cup cocoa powder, Dutch-processed
- ¾ cup all-purpose flour
- 1 tsp. vanilla extract
- 1 whole egg
- 1 egg white
- 1/3 cup buttermilk
- 1 oz. chocolate, dark melted
- 4 tbsp. butter, melted
Cream cheese frosting
- 8 oz. cream cheese, softened
- 1 stick butter, softened
- 2 tsp. vanilla extract
- ½ cup cocoa powder, Dutch-processed
- 3 cups sugar, powdered
Procedure:
1. Preheat the oven to 350°F.
2. Use paper liners on 12 cupcake tins.
3. Combine the salt, baking soda, baking powder, cinnamon, cardamom, sugar, cocoa, and all-purpose flour in a large bowl. Set aside.
4. Attach the whisk fitting to the electric mixer.
5. Pour the vanilla, egg, egg white, buttermilk, chocolate, and butter in a mixing bowl.
6. Set the mixer on medium, and whisk the butter mixture until thoroughly combined.

7. Set the mixer on low, and gradually whisk in the flour mixture. Remember to occasionally scrape the sides of the bowl.
8. Once the batter has thoroughly combined, pour it into each lined cupcake tin. Make sure that the tins are only three-quarters full.
9. Bake for 20 minutes.
10. Remove from oven, and let cool for 10 minutes.
11. Remove the cupcakes from the tins, and place them on a wire rack to cool completely.
12. While waiting for the cupcakes to cool, make the cream cheese frosting. To start, place the cream cheese and butter in a mixing bowl.
13. Set the mixer on medium, on beat the butter mixture together.
14. Whisk in the vanilla extract.
15. Set the mixer on low, and gradually add the cocoa and sugar.
16. Once the frosting is fluffy, turn off the mixer.
17. Use a spatula or pastry bag to top the cupcakes with the cream cheese.
18. Bon appétit!

Orange Spiced Chai Cupcakes with Vanilla Spiced Butter Cream

Ingredients:
Orange spiced chai cupcakes

- ½ tsp. nutmeg, ground (
- 1 tsp. ginger, grated
- 2 tsp. cinnamon, ground
- ½ tsp. salt
- 1 tsp. baking soda
- 1 tsp. baking powder
- 2 ½ cups cake flour, sifted
- 1 cup sugar, granulated (
- ½ cup sugar, brown (
- 1 orange, zested
- ¼ cup water(
- 2 chai tea bags(
- ½ cup orange juice
- ½ cup buttermilk(
- 1 tsp. vanilla extract(
- 2 whole eggs(
- 1/3 cup vegetable oil(
  Vanilla spice butter cream
- 1 cup butter, unsalted, and softened(
- 6 cups sugar, powdered (
- 1/8 tsp. nutmeg, ground (
- 1/8 tsp. ginger, ground (
- 1 tsp. cinnamon, ground (
- 2 tsp. vanilla extract
  Procedure:
1. Preheat the oven to 350°F.
2. Use paper liners on 12 cupcake tins.
3. In a large bowl, combine the nutmeg, ginger, cinnamon, salt, baking soda, baking powder, and flour. Set aside.
4. In a separate bowl, use your hands to rub together the sugars and zest. Set aside.

40

5. Pour the water in a saucepan.
6. Place the pan over a stove set on medium.
7. Once the water begins to simmer, submerge the tea bags.
8. After 5 minutes, remove the bags, and set the tea aside to cool completely.
9. Once cooled, stir together the tea, orange juice, and buttermilk. Set aside.
10. Attach the whisk fitting to the electric mixer.
11. Place the vanilla extract, eggs, oil, and prepared sugars in a mixing bowl.
12. Set the mixer on high, and whisk the mixture together for 5 minutes. Remember to occasionally scrape the sides of the bowl.
13. Set the mixer on low, and alternately whisk in the flour and tea mixtures.
14. Once the batter has thoroughly combined, pour it into each lined cupcake tin. Make sure that the tins are only three-quarters full.
15. Bake for 15 minutes.
16. Remove from oven, and let cool for 10 minutes.
17. Remove the cupcakes from the tins, and place them on a wire rack to cool completely.
18. While waiting for the cupcakes to cool, make the butter cream. To start, use an electric mixer to beat the butter for a few minutes.
19. Set the mixer on medium. Beat in 4 cups of sugar, followed by the nutmeg, ginger, cinnamon, and finally the vanilla.
20. Gradually pour in the remaining sugar until the frosting reaches the desired consistency.
21. Once the cupcakes have cooled, frost them with the butter cream.
22. Enjoy!

Chocolate and Bacon Cupcakes in Maple Frosting

Ingredients:
Cupcakes
- ¾ cup cocoa powder, unsweetened, and Dutch-processed
- ¾ cup water, hot
- 1 ¼ tsp. salt
- 1 tsp. baking powder
- 1 tsp. baking soda
- 3 cups all-purpose flour
- 1 ½ cups butter, unsalted
- 2 ¼ cups sugar
- 4 whole eggs
- 1 tbsp. plus 1 tsp. vanilla extract
- 1 cup sour cream, softened
- ¾ cup bacon, cooked, and crumbled
Maple frosting
- 2 sticks butter, unsalted, and softened
- 2 tsp. vanilla extract
- 1 lb. sugar, confectioners'
- 1/3 cup maple syrup
- 1 tsp. salt

- Maple syrup to drizzle

Procedure:
1. Preheat the oven to 350°F.
2. Use paper liners on 24 cupcake tins.
3. Pour the hot water in a small bowl, and stir in the cocoa. Set aside.
4. Sift together the salt, baking powder, baking soda, and flour in a separate bowl. Set aside.
5. Place the butter in a saucepan.
6. Melt the butter over low heat, and stir in the sugar.
7. Pour the resulting mixture into a mixing bowl.
8. Attach the whisk fitting to the electric mixer.
9. Set the mixer on medium-low, and whisk the butter mixture for 5 minutes.
10. Beat the eggs in one at a time. Remember to occasionally scrape the sides of the bowl.
11. Whisk in the cocoa mixture and the vanilla.
12. Set the mixer on low, and alternately whisk in the flour and sour cream.
13. Turn off the mixer, and fold in the bacon bits.
14. Once the batter has thoroughly combined, pour it into each lined cupcake tin. Make sure that the tins are only three-quarters full.
15. Bake for 20 minutes.
16. Remove from oven, and let cool for 10 minutes.
17. Remove the cupcakes from the tins, and place them on a wire rack to cool completely.
18. While waiting for the cupcakes to cool, make the maple frosting. To start, place the butter in a mixing bowl.
19. Attach the whisk fitting to the electric mixer.
20. Set the mixer on medium, and whisk the butter for a few minutes.
21. Whisk in the maple syrup, salt, and vanilla extract until thoroughly combined.

22. Gradually whisk in the sugar, and adjust the sweetness with maple syrup to taste.
23. Once the frosting is fluffy, turn off the mixer.
24. Use a spatula or pastry bag to top the cupcakes with the frosting.
25. Sprinkle with bacon bits, and drizzle on additional maple syrup.

Ginger Cupcakes in Ginger Cream Cheese

Ingredients:
Ginger cupcakes
- ¼ tsp. salt
- 1 tsp. baking powder
- 1 tbsp. ginger, ground
- ¾ cup ginger, candied, and chopped
- 1 ½ cups all-purpose flour
- ½ cup butter, unsalted, and softened
- 1 ¼ cups sugar, granulated
- 3 whole eggs
- ¾ cup milk
  Ginger cream cheese
- ¼ cup butter, unsalted, and softened

- 4 oz. cream cheese, softened
- 2 ¼ cups sugar, confectioners'
- ¼ tsp. salt
- 1 tsp. ginger, ground
- ¼ cup ginger, crystallized, and chopped

Procedure:
1. Preheat the oven to 350°F.
2. Use paper liners on 12 cupcake tins.
3. Whisk together the salt, baking powder, ground ginger, candied ginger and flour in a large bowl. Set aside.
4. Place the butter and sugar in a mixing bowl.
5. Attach the whisk fitting to the electric mixer.
6. Whisk together the butter mixture until thoroughly combined.
7. Beat in the eggs one at a time.
8. Set the mixer on low, and alternately whisk in the prepared flour mixture and milk.
9. Once the batter has thoroughly combined, pour it into each lined cupcake tin. Make sure that the tins are only three-quarters full.
10. Bake for 25 minutes.
11. Remove from oven, and let cool for 10 minutes.
12. Remove the cupcakes from the tins, and place them on a wire rack to cool completely.
13. While waiting for the cupcakes to cool, make the cream cheese. To start, place the butter and cream cheese in a mixing bowl.
14. Set the mixer on medium-high, and whisk the butter mixture together for a few minutes.
15. Set the mixer on low, and gradually whisk in the sugar.
16. Set the mixer on medium-high, and whisk in the remaining ingredients one at a time.
17. Once the frosting is fluffy, turn off the mixer.

18. Use a spatula or pastry bag to top the cupcakes with the frosting.
19. Refrigerate until ready to enjoy.

Cookies and Cream Cupcakes

Ingredients:
Cupcakes
- 2 cups sugar
- 1 ¾ cups all-purpose flour
- ¾ cup cocoa powder, Dutch-processed
- 1 ½ tsp. baking powder
- 1 ½ tsp. baking soda
- 1 tsp. salt
- 2 whole eggs
- 1 cup milk
- ½ cup vegetable oil
- 2 tsp. vanilla extract
- 1 cup water, boiling
Cookies and cream frosting
- 2 cups whipping cream
- 4 tbsp. sugar, powdered

- 1 tsp. vanilla extract
- 12 Oreos, crushed
- 12 halved Oreos for garnish

Procedure:
1. Preheat the oven to 350°F.
2. Use paper liners on 12 cupcake tins.
3. Whisk together the salt, baking soda, baking powder, cocoa, flour, and sugar in a large bowl. Set aside.
4. Attach the whisk fitting to the electric mixer.
5. Place the vanilla, oil, milk, and eggs in a mixing bowl.
6. Set the mixer on medium, and whisk the egg mixture together for 2 minutes.
7. Set the mixer on low, and gradually whisk in the flour.
8. Set the mixer on medium, and whisk in the water.
9. Once the batter has thoroughly combined, pour it into each lined cupcake tin. Make sure that the tins are only three-quarters full.
10. Bake for 25 minutes.
11. Remove from oven, and let cool for 10 minutes.
12. Remove the cupcakes from the tins, and place them on a wire rack to cool completely.
13. While waiting for the cupcakes to cool, make the frosting. To start, place the vanilla, sugar, and whipping cream in a mixing bowl.
14. Set the mixer on medium, and whisk together the ingredients for 5 minutes.
15. Once the frosting forms stiff peaks, turn off the mixer.
16. Gently fold in the crushed Oreos.
17. Use a spatula or pastry bag to top the cupcakes with the frosting.
18. Use the Oreos halves for garnish.

Sweet Potato Cupcakes

Ingredients:
- ¼ tsp. ginger, ground
- ¼ tsp. cloves
- ½ tsp. cinnamon, ground
- ½ tsp. salt
- ½ tsp. baking soda
- 2 tsp. baking powder
- 2 cups all-purpose flour
- ¾ cup milk
- 1/3 cup butter, melted
- 2/3 cup sugar, brown
- 1 whole egg
- 1 egg yolk
- 1 cup sweet potato, pureed
- 2 tbsp. maple syrup

Procedure:
1. Preheat the oven to 400°F.
2. Use paper liners on 12 cupcake tins.
3. In a large bowl, combine the ginger, cloves, cinnamon, salt, baking soda, baking powder, and flour. Set aside.

4. Place the milk, butter, sugar, egg, and egg yolk in a mixing bowl.
5. Attach the whisk fitting to the electric mixer.
6. Set the mixer on medium, and whisk the ingredients together for a few minutes.
7. Whisk in the sweet potato and maple syrup.
8. Set the mixer on low, and gradually whisk in the flour mixture.
9. Once the batter has thoroughly combined, pour it into each lined cupcake tin. Make sure that the tins are only three-quarters full.
10. Bake for 20 minutes.
11. Remove from oven, and let cool for 10 minutes.
12. Remove the cupcakes from the tins, and place them on a wire rack to cool completely.
13. Frost and garnish as desired. These cupcakes are fairly versatile and will go well with most types of frosting.

Sour Cream Apple Cupcakes

Ingredients:
Cupcakes
- ¼ tsp. salt
- 1 tsp. baking soda
- 1 ½ tsp. baking powder

- 2 cups all-purpose flour
- 1 cup sugar
- ½ cup butter, unsalted, and softened
- 2 whole eggs
- 1 cup sour cream
- 1 tsp. vanilla extract
  Apple topping
- 2 cups apples, chopped
- ½ cup walnuts, chopped
- ¼ cup sugar, brown
- 1 tbsp. butter, unsalted, and melted
- 1 tbsp. all-purpose flour
- 1 tsp. cinnamon

Procedure:
1. Preheat the oven to 400°F.
2. Use paper liners on 12 cupcake tins.
3. In a large bowl, combine the salt, baking soda, baking powder, and flour. Set aside.
4. Place the sugar and butter in a mixing bowl.
5. Attach the whisk fitting to the electric mixer.
6. Set the mixer on medium, and whisk the butter mixture together for a few minutes.
7. Beat in the eggs one at a time.
8. Whisk in the sour cream and vanilla.
9. Set the mixer on low, and whisk in the flour mixture until smooth.
10. Pour the half of the batter equally into each lined cupcake tin. Set aside.
11. In a small bowl, stir together all the topping ingredients.
12. Sprinkle half of the topping mixture over the cupcakes.
13. Pour the remaining half of the batter into the tins.
14. Sprinkle the remaining half of the topping mixture over the cupcakes.

15. Bake until a tester comes out clean. This should take around 20 minutes.
16. Enjoy warm.

Orange Clove Cupcakes in Vanilla Butter Cream

Ingredients:
Candied orange peel
- 2 oranges
- 1 tbsp. salt
- ½ tsp. cloves, ground
- 3 cups sugar
- Water as needed
Cupcakes
- ½ tsp. salt
- 1 tbsp. baking powder
- 1 ½ tsp. cloves, ground
- 2 tbsp. orange zest, grated
- 3 cups all-purpose flour
- 5 whole eggs
- 1 ½ cups sugar
- 1 tbsp. vanilla extract
- 1 cup vegetable oil

- ¾ cup orange juice
  Vanilla butter cream
- 1 cup butter, softened
- 4 cups sugar, powdered
- ¼ cup milk
- 1 tsp. vanilla extract
  Procedure:
1. Use a vegetable peeler to cut the peel into long thin strips.
2. Remove any white pith that's attached to the peel.
3. Pour 4 cups of water into a small bowl.
4. Stir in the salt and orange peel.
5. Let stand for 8 hours.
6. Place the peels in a saucepan, and drain the water.
7. Pour enough cold water into the pan to cover the peels. Boil the water over high heat, then immediately drain the water. Repeat this step 3 times.
8. After the last repetition, add ½ cup of water into the pan.
9. Stir in 2 cups of sugar.
10. Let cook over medium heat, until the peel begins to turn translucent.
11. Drain any excess liquid in the pan.
12. Stir together the cloves and sugar in a small bowl.
13. Coat the orange peels with the clove mixture.
14. Let dry, and refrigerate in an airtight container until ready to use.
15. Preheat the oven to 350°F.
16. Use paper liners on 24 cupcake tins.
17. In a large bowl, whisk together the salt, baking powder, cloves, zest, and flour. Set aside.
18. Place the eggs and sugar in a mixing bowl.
19. Attach the whisk fitting to the mixer.
20. Set the mixer on high, and mix the egg mixture for half a minute.
21. Once the mixture is fluffy, whisk in the oil and vanilla.

22. Set the mixer on low, and alternately whisk in the flour mixture and orange juice.
23. Once the batter has thoroughly combined, pour it into each lined cupcake tin. Make sure that the tins are only three-quarters full.
24. Bake for 20 minutes.
25. Remove from oven, and let cool for 10 minutes.
26. Remove the cupcakes from the tins, and place them on a wire rack to cool completely.
27. While waiting for the cupcakes to cool, make the butter cream. To start, place the butter in a mixing bowl.
28. Set the mixer on medium, and beat the butter until it softens.
29. Beat in the remaining ingredients.
30. Once thoroughly combined, frost the cooled cupcakes with the butter cream.

Snickers Cupcake

Ingredients:
Cupcakes
- 2 cups sugar
- 1 ¾ cups all-purpose flour
- ¾ cup cocoa powder, Dutch-processed
- 1 ½ tsp. baking powder

- 1 ½ tsp. baking soda
- ½ tsp. salt
- 2 tsp. vanilla extract
- ½ cup vegetable oil
- 1 cup milk
- 2 whole eggs
- 1 cup water, boiling
- Caramel sauce as needed
  Frosting
- 1 cup butter, unsalted, and softened
- ¼ cup caramel sauce
- ¼ cup heavy cream
- 1 tsp. vanilla extract
- 1 lb. sugar, powdered
- 8 chopped mini Snickers bars

Procedure:
1. Preheat the oven to 350°F.
2. Use paper liners on 30 cupcake tins.
3. Place the salt and sugar in a mixing bowl.
4. Attach the whisk fitting to the electric mixer.
5. Set the mixer on low, and whisk in the vanilla, oil, milk, and eggs.
6. Set the mixer on medium, and continue whisking for another 2 minutes.
7. Whisk in the boiling water.
8. Once the batter has thoroughly combined, pour it into each lined cupcake tin. Make sure that the tins are only three-quarters full.
9. Bake for 22 minutes.
10. Remove from oven, and let cool for 10 minutes.
11. Remove the cupcakes from the tins, and place them on a wire rack to cool completely.

12. Use a small cookie cutter to remove the center of each cupcake. Make sure the hole is around two-thirds of the cupcake in depth.
13. Pipe caramel sauce into each cupcake center until full. Set aside.
14. Place the butter in a mixing bowl.
15. Set the mixer on medium, and beat the butter for 2 minutes.
16. Whisk in the vanilla, heavy cream, and caramel sauce.
17. Set the mixer on low, and whisk in just enough sugar to achieve the desired consistency.
18. Set the mixer on medium-high, and continue whisking for another minute.
19. Once the frosting is fluffy, turn off the mixer.
20. Use a spatula or pastry bag to top the cupcakes with the frosting.
21. Garnish with the chopped Snickers bars.

Butter Banana Rum Cupcakes

Ingredients:
Butter banana rum cupcakes
- 2 cups flour
- 3 tsp. baking powder
- ¼ tsp. baking soda
- ¼ tsp. salt
- ¾ cup sugar, brown

- 10 tbsp. butter, unsalted, and softened
- 4 whole eggs
- ¾ cup sugar
- 1 tsp. vanilla
- ½ tsp. rum flavoring
- 1 cup milk
- 2 bananas, ripe, and mashed
  Butter penuche frosting
- 1/2 cup butter, unsalted, and softened
- 1 cup sugar, brown
- ¼ cup buttermilk, heated
- ½ tsp. vanilla
- 3 cups sugar, confectioners'
- 1 ½ cups pecans, chopped
- 1 cup coconut flakes

Procedure:
1. Preheat the oven to 325°F.
2. Use paper liners on 16 cupcake tins.
3. Combine the brown sugar, salt, baking soda, baking powder, and flour in a large bowl. Set aside.
4. Place the butter in a saucepan.
5. Brown the butter over medium heat.
6. Once browned, strain the butter, and let stand to cool.
7. Place the eggs and sugar in a mixing bowl.
8. Attach the paddle fitting to the electric mixer.
9. Set the mixer on medium-high, and whisk the egg mixture together until fluffy.
10. Whisk in the butter, followed by the vanilla, and the rum flavouring.
11. Set the mixer on medium, and beat in the mashed bananas.
12. Set the mixer on low, and alternately beat in the flour and milk.

13. Once the batter has thoroughly combined, pour it into each lined cupcake tin. Make sure that the tins are only three-quarters full.
14. Bake for 20 minutes.
15. Remove from oven, and let cool for 10 minutes.
16. Remove the cupcakes from the tins, and place them on a wire rack to cool completely.
17. While waiting for the cupcakes to cool, make the penuche frosting. To start, brown the butter in a saucepan.
18. Stir in the brown sugar until it melts.
19. Remove the mixture from the heat.
20. Stir in the buttermilk.
21. Once thoroughly combined, let stand to cool.
22. Place the mixture in a mixing bowl.
23. Set the mixer on low.
24. Beat in the vanilla and confectioners' sugar.
25. Beat in the coconut flakes and pecans.
26. Pour a spoonful of the frosting over each cooled cupcake.
27. Garnish pecan halves and coconut flakes, if desired.

Cherry Coke Float Cupcakes

Ingredients:

Cupcakes
- 1 ½ cups flour
- ¾ cup sugar
- ½ tsp. baking soda
- ¼ tsp. salt
- 1 whole egg
- ½ cup buttermilk
- 2 tsp. vanilla
- ½ cup butter, unsalted, and softened
- 3 tbsp. cocoa powder, Dutch-processed
- ¾ cup Coca-Cola
- ¼ cup maraschino cherry syrup
- 24 maraschino cherries
- Whipped cream
- Chocolate syrup

Procedure:
1. Preheat the oven to 350°F.
2. Use paper liners on 12 cupcake tins.
3. Sift together the salt, baking soda, sugar, and flour in a large bowl. Set aside.
4. In a separate bowl, stir together the vanilla, buttermilk, and egg.
5. Pour the Coca-Cola into a saucepan.
6. Place the pan over a stove set on medium.
7. Bring the soda to a boil, and whisk in the cherry syrup.
8. Whisk in the cocoa powder and butter.
9. Pour the contents of the pan into a mixing bowl.
10. Attach the paddle fitting to the electric mixer.
11. Set the mixer on low, and gradually beat in the flour mixture.
12. Once the batter has thoroughly combined, pour it into each lined cupcake tin. Make sure that the tins are only three-quarters full.
13. Push a cherry into the batter.
14. Bake for 15 minutes.

15. Remove from oven, and let cool for 10 minutes.
16. Remove the cupcakes from the tins, and place them on a wire rack to cool completely.
17. Once cooled completely, top the cupcakes with whipped cream.
18. Drizzle chocolate syrup over the cream.
19. Garnish with a cherry.

Lemon Meringue Cupcakes

Ingredients:
- ½ tsp. salt
- 1 tbsp. baking powder
- 3 cups all-purpose flour
- 1 cup buttermilk
- 2 tbsp. lemon juice
- 2 cups sugar
- 1 cup butter, unsalted, and softened
- 4 whole eggs
- 1 tsp. vanilla extract
- 3 tbsp. lemon zest
- Lemon curd as needed
- Seven-minute frosting as needed

Procedure:
1. Preheat the oven to 325°F.

2. Use paper liners on 12 cupcake tins.
3. Sift together the salt, baking powder, and flour in a large bowl. Set aside.
4. Stir together the buttermilk and lemon juice in a separate bowl. Set aside.
5. Place the sugar and butter in a mixing bowl.
6. Attach the paddle fitting to the electric mixer.
7. Set the mixer on medium-high, and beat the butter mixture until fluffy.
8. Beat the eggs in one a time. Remember to occasionally scrape the sides of the bowl.
9. Beat in the vanilla and lemon zest.
10. Set the mixer on low, and alternately beat in the flour and buttermilk mixtures.
11. Once the batter has thoroughly combined, pour it into each lined cupcake tin. Make sure that the tins are only three-quarters full.
12. Push a cherry into the batter.
13. Bake for 25 minutes.
14. Remove from oven, and let cool for 10 minutes.
15. Remove the cupcakes from the tins, and place them on a wire rack to cool completely.
16. Brush lemon curd on each cooled cupcake.
17. Make the seven-minute frosting according to the instructions on the pack.
18. Attach an open-star tip to a pastry bag.
19. Pipe the frosting through the pastry bag, and follow the design as pictured.
20. Wave a kitchen torch back and forth 4 inches away from the frosting.
21. Once the frosting has browned lightly, the cupcakes are ready to serve.

Apple Pie Cupcakes

Ingredients:
Apple topping
- 3 tbsp. butter, unsalted, and softened
- 1/3 cup sugar, granulated
- 3 apples, peeled, cored, and sliced
  Cupcakes
- ¼ tsp. salt
- 1 tsp. cinnamon, ground
- 2 ¼ tsp. baking powder
- 2 ¼ cups all-purpose flour
- 1 ½ cups sugar, granulated
- 9 oz. butter, unsalted, and softened
- 4 whole eggs
- ½ tsp. lemon zest
- ½ tsp. vanilla extract
- 8 oz. milk
  Cinnamon frosting
- 12 oz. butter, unsalted, and softened
- ½ tsp. cinnamon, ground
- 1 ½ cups sugar, confectioners'

Procedure:
1. Place the butter in a skillet.

2. Place the skillet over a stove set on medium-low.
3. Stir in the sugar to dissolve.
4. Cook the apple slices in the butter for 10 minutes.
5. Remove the skillet from the heat, and set aside to cool.
6. Preheat the oven to 325°F.
7. Use paper liners on 24 cupcake tins.
8. Sift together the salt, cinnamon, baking powder, and flour in a large bowl. Set aside.
9. Place the sugar and butter in a mixing bowl.
10. Attach the paddle fitting to the electric mixer.
11. Set the mixer on medium, and beat the butter mixture until fluffy.
12. Beat in the eggs one at a time. Remember to occasionally scrape the sides of the bowl.
13. Whisk in the zest and vanilla.
14. Set the mixer on low, and alternately beat in the flour mixture and milk.
15. Once the batter has thoroughly combined, pour it into each lined cupcake tin. Make sure that the tins are only three-quarters full.
16. Bake for 20 minutes.
17. Remove from oven, and let cool for 10 minutes.
18. Remove the cupcakes from the tins, and place them on a wire rack to cool completely.
19. While waiting for the cupcakes to cool, it's time to make the frosting. To start, place the butter in a mixing bowl.
20. Set the mixer on medium, and beat the butter for 3 minutes.
21. Beat in the cinnamon and sugar for another 5 minutes.
22. Once the frosting is fluffy, turn off the mixer.
23. Use a spatula or pastry bag to top the cupcakes with the frosting.
24. Sprinkle additional ground cinnamon over the frosting.

Cream Soda and Toffee Cupcakes

Ingredients:
- ¼ tsp. salt
- ½ tsp. baking soda
- 1 ½ tsp. baking powder
- 2 cups all-purpose flour
- ½ cup cream soda
- ½ cup buttermilk
- ½ cup butter, softened
- ¼ cup sugar, brown
- ¾ cup sugar, granulated
- 3 whole eggs
- 1 ½ tsp. vanilla
- 1 tbsp. molasses
- ¾ cup toffee pieces

Procedure:
1. Preheat the oven to 325°F.
2. Use paper liners on 18 cupcake tins.
3. Sift together the salt, baking soda, baking powder, and flour in a large bowl. Set aside.
4. Combine the cream soda and buttermilk in a separate bowl. Set aside.

5. Place the butter in a mixing bowl.
6. Attach the paddle fitting to the electric mixer.
7. Set the mixer on high, and beat the butter for half a minute.
8. Gradually beat in the sugars.
9. Set the mixer on low, and whisk in the eggs one at a time.
10. Whisk in the vanilla and molasses.
11. Alternately whisk in the flour and buttermilk mixtures.
12. Beat in half a cup of toffee pieces.
13. Once the batter has thoroughly combined, pour it into each lined cupcake tin. Make sure that the tins are only three-quarters full.
14. Bake for 18 minutes.
15. Remove from oven, and let cool for 10 minutes.
16. Remove the cupcakes from the tins, and place them on a wire rack to cool completely.
17. Once cooled completely, frost, and garnish with the leftover toffee.

White Chocolate Raspberry Cupcakes

Ingredients:
Cupcakes
- ½ tsp. salt
- ¼ tsp. baking soda
- tsp. baking powder
- ½ cup sugar, granulated

- ¼ cup sugar, brown
- 1 ¼ cups all-purpose flour
- 1/3 cup vegetable oil
- 4 oz. chocolate, white, and melted
- 2 tsp. vanilla extract
- ½ tsp. lemon zest, grated
- ½ cup milk, coconut
- ½ cup milk, soy
  Filling
- 1 tsp. lemon juice
- 3 tbsp. sugar
- 1 tbsp. water
- 8 oz. raspberries, frozen
- ¼ cup water with 1 tbsp. cornstarch
  Frosting
- 1/3 cup cream cheese, softened
- ½ cup butter, softened
- 3 ½ cup sugar, confectioners'
- 1 tsp. vanilla extract
- 6 oz. chocolate, white, and melted
- 1 tbsp. milk, soy
- 12 raspberries for garnish
  Procedure:
1. Preheat the oven to 350°F.
2. Use paper liners on 12 cupcake tins.
3. Combine the salt, baking soda, baking powder, sugars, and flour in a bowl. Set aside.
4. In a separate bowl, whisk together the oil and chocolate.
5. Whisk in the vanilla, zest, and milks.
6. Pour the chocolate mixture into the bowl of flour. Whisk together until smooth.
7. Once the batter has thoroughly combined, pour it into each lined cupcake tin. Make sure that the tins are only three-quarters full.
8. Bake for 25 minutes.

9. Remove from oven, and let cool for 10 minutes.
10. Remove the cupcakes from the tins, and place them on a wire rack to cool completely.
11. While waiting for the cupcakes to cool, make the raspberry filling. To start, place the lemon juice, sugar, water, and raspberries in a saucepan.
12. Place the pan over a stove set on medium.
13. Stir in 1 tbsp. of the cornstarch mixture, and bring the filling to a simmer.
14. Place a fine sieve over a medium bowl.
15. Strain the mixture through the sieve. Discard the solids.
16. Pour the strained mixture back into the pan, and place it back on the stove.
17. Add another tbsp. of the cornstarch mixture, and let simmer for a few more minutes.
18. Remove the pan from the heat, and set aside to cool.
19. Use a small cookie cutter to remove the center of each cupcake. Make sure the hole is around two-thirds of the cupcake in depth.
20. Pipe the raspberry filling into each cupcake center until full. Set aside.
21. Place the cream cheese and butter in a mixing bowl.
22. Set the mixer on medium, and whisk the two together until fluffy.
23. Gradually whisk in the sugar.
24. Stir together the vanilla and chocolate in a separate bowl.
25. Beat in the chocolate mixture and soy milk.
26. Once the frosting is fluffy, turn off the mixer.
27. Use a spatula or pastry bag to top the cupcakes with the frosting.
28. Garnish each frosted cupcake with a fresh raspberry.

Easy Cupcake Recipes

Vanilla Lemon Cupcakes

Prep Time: 35 minutes
Servings: 12
Ingredients:
3 cups self-rising flour
1/2 teaspoon salt
1 cup unsalted butter, softened
2 cups white sugar
4 eggs, room temperature
1 teaspoon vanilla extract
2 tablespoons lemon zest
1 cup whole milk, divided
2 1/2 tablespoons fresh lemon juice, divided

Directions:
1. Set oven to 375 degrees.
2. Combine butter and sugar in a bowl using an electric mixer.
3. Gradually add the eggs in, one egg at a time and then add vanilla extract and lemon zest.

4. Slowly add flour and salt, alternating between milk and lemon juice.
5. Mix well and pour into a cupcake tin. Bake for 15-17 minutes.

Double Chocolate Cupcakes

Prep Time: 45 minutes
Servings: 12

Ingredients:
1 1/2 cups flour
1 teaspoon baking soda
1/4 cup cocoa powder
1/2 teaspoon salt
1 cup white sugar
1/3 cup vegetable oil
1 cup water
1 tablespoon vinegar
1 teaspoon vanilla extract

Directions:
1. Set oven to 350 degrees.
2. Combine flour, baking soda, salt and cocoa powder.
3. In another bowl, combine oil, water and 1 cup of sugar.
4. Add vanilla and vinegar and slowly add flour mixture.
5. Pour batter into a cupcake pan and bake for 20-25 minutes.

Carrot Cupcakes

Prep Time: 30 minutes

Servings: 12
Ingredients:
2 eggs, lightly beaten
1 1/8 cups white sugar
1/3 cup brown sugar
1/2 cup vegetable oil
1 teaspoon vanilla extract
2 cups shredded carrots
1/2 cup crushed pineapple
1 1/2 cups all-purpose flour
1 1/4 teaspoons baking soda
1/2 teaspoon salt
1 1/2 teaspoons ground cinnamon
1/2 teaspoon ground nutmeg
1/4 teaspoon ground ginger
1 cup chopped walnut

Directions:
1. Set oven to 350 degrees.
2. Beat eggs, white sugar, brown sugar and oil in a bowl with vanilla.
3. Add carrots and pineapple.
4. In another bowl, combine baking soda, flour and salt with nutmeg, cinnamon and ginger.
5. Combine both bowls and add walnuts.
6. Mix thoroughly and pour mixture into a cupcake tin.
7. Bake for 15-20 minutes.

Red Velvet Cupcakes

Prep Time: 35 minutes
Servings: 12
Ingredients:

2 1/2 cups flour
1/2 cup unsweetened cocoa powder
1 teaspoon baking soda
1/2 teaspoon salt
1 cup butter, softened
2 cups sugar
4 eggs
1 cup sour cream
1/2 cup milk
1 bottle red food color
2 teaspoons pure vanilla extract

Directions:
1. Set oven to 350 degrees.
2. Combine all wet ingredients together in a bowl and mix thoroughly.
3. In another bowl, mix dry ingredients.
4. Gradually combine both bowls together and pour into cupcake tin.
5. Bake for 15-20 minutes.

Easy Chocolate Cupcakes

Prep Time: 45 minutes
Servings: 12
Ingredients:
1 1/3 cups all-purpose flour
1/4 teaspoon baking soda
2 teaspoons baking powder
3/4 cup unsweetened cocoa powder
1/8 teaspoon salt
3 tablespoons butter, softened
1 1/2 cups white sugar

2 eggs
3/4 teaspoon vanilla extract
1 cup milk

Directions:
1. Set oven to 350 degrees.
2. Combine all wet ingredients, except eggs, together in a bowl and mix thoroughly.
3. In another bowl, mix dry ingredients.
4. Gradually combine both bowls together and pour into cupcake tin.
5. Gradually beat eggs into the mixture, one egg at a time.
6. Bake for 15-20 minutes.

Gingerbread Cupcakes

Prep Time: 35 minutes
Servings: 12
Ingredients:
5 tablespoons unsalted butter, softened
1/2 cup white sugar
1/2 cup molasses
1 egg
1 egg yolk
1 1/4 cups flour
1 tablespoon cocoa powder
1 1/4 teaspoons ground ginger
1 teaspoon ground cinnamon
1/2 teaspoon ground allspice
1/2 teaspoon ground nutmeg
1/4 teaspoon salt
1 teaspoon baking soda
1/2 cup hot milk
2 tablespoons unsalted butter, softened

2 ounces cream cheese, softened
2/3 cup sifted confectioners' sugar
1/4 teaspoon lemon extract

Directions:
1. Set oven to 350 degrees.
2. Combine all wet ingredients, except eggs, together in a bowl and mix thoroughly.
3. In another bowl, mix dry ingredients.
4. Gradually combine both bowls together and pour into cupcake tin.
5. Gradually beat eggs into the mixture, one egg at a time.
6. Bake for 15-20 minutes.

Vanilla Cream Cupcakes

Prep Time: 35 minutes
Servings: 12
Ingredients:
1 cup white sugar
1/2 cup butter
2 eggs
1 1/2 teaspoons vanilla extract
1 1/2 cups all-purpose flour
1 3/4 teaspoons baking powder
1/2 cup milk

Directions:
1. Set oven to 350 degrees.
2. Combine all wet ingredients, except eggs, together in a bowl and mix thoroughly.
3. In another bowl, mix dry ingredients.
4. Gradually combine both bowls together and pour into cupcake tin.

5. Gradually beat eggs into the mixture, one egg at a time.
6. Bake for 15-20 minutes.

Almond Cupcakes

Prep Time: 35 minutes
Servings: 12
Ingredients:
1 1/2 cups almond flour
1 3/4 teaspoons baking powder
1 cup white sugar
1/2 cup butter, softened
2 eggs
1 teaspoon vanilla extract
1 teaspoon almond extract
3/4 cup whole milk

Directions:
1. Set oven to 350 degrees.
2. Combine all wet ingredients, except eggs, together in a bowl and mix thoroughly.
3. In another bowl, mix dry ingredients.
4. Gradually combine both bowls together and pour into cupcake tin.
5. Gradually beat eggs into the mixture, one egg at a time.
6. Bake for 15-20 minutes.

Banana Cupcake

Prep Time: 45 minutes
Servings: 12
Ingredients:
2 cups flour
1 teaspoon baking soda
1 teaspoon salt
1/2 teaspoon ground cinnamon
1/2 teaspoon ground nutmeg

2/3 cup shortening
1 1/4 cups white sugar
2 eggs
1 teaspoon vanilla extract
1/4 cup buttermilk
1 cup ripe bananas, mashed
2 apples, peeled, cored and grated

Directions:
1. Set oven to 350 degrees.
2. Combine all wet ingredients, except eggs and fruits, together in a bowl and mix thoroughly.
3. In another bowl, mix dry ingredients.
4. Gradually combine both bowls together and pour into cupcake tin.
5. Gradually beat eggs into the mixture, one egg at a time. Once mixed, fold in fruits and mix until well blended.
6. Bake for 15-20 minutes.

Peanut Butter Cupcake

Prep Time: 45 minutes
Servings: 12
Ingredients:
2 cups brown sugar
1/2 cup shortening
1 cup peanut butter
2 eggs
1 1/2 cups milk
1 teaspoon vanilla extract
2 1/2 cups flour
1 teaspoon baking soda
2 teaspoons cream of tartar
1 pinch salt

Directions:
1. Set oven to 350 degrees.
2. Combine all wet ingredients, except eggs, together in a bowl and mix thoroughly.
3. In another bowl, mix dry ingredients.
4. Gradually combine both bowls together and pour into cupcake tin.
5. Gradually beat eggs into the mixture, one egg at a time.
6. Bake for 15-20 minutes.

Chocolate Chip Cupcakes

Prep Time: 45 minutes
Servings: 12
Ingredients:

1 package brownie mix
2 eggs
1/2 cup vegetable oil
1/4 cup water
1 1/2 cups semi-sweet chocolate chips

Directions:
1. Set oven to 350 degrees.
2. Combine all wet ingredients, except eggs, together in a bowl and mix thoroughly.
3. In another bowl, mix dry ingredients.
4. Gradually combine both bowls together and pour into cupcake tin.
5. Gradually beat eggs into the mixture, one egg at a time; and fold in chocolate chips.
6. Bake for 15-20 minutes.

Brownie Cupcakes

Prep Time: 30 minutes
Servings: 12
Ingredients:
1 cup butter
1 cup chocolate chips
4 eggs
1 1/2 cups white sugar
1 cup flour
1 teaspoon vanilla extract

Directions:
1. Set oven to 350 degrees.
2. Combine all wet ingredients, except eggs, together in a bowl and mix thoroughly.
3. In another bowl, mix dry ingredients.
4. Gradually combine both bowls together and pour into cupcake tin.
5. Gradually beat eggs into the mixture, one egg at a time.
6. Bake for 15-20 minutes.

Vanilla Coconut Cupcakes

Prep Time: 45 minutes
Servings: 12
Ingredients:
1 1/4 cups all-purpose flour
3/4 teaspoon baking soda
1 pinch salt
5 tablespoons butter, cut into chunks
2/3 cup milk
1 cup white sugar
2 eggs

1 egg yolk
1 teaspoon vanilla extract
1/2 cup coconut, shredded

Directions:
1. Set oven to 350 degrees.
2. Combine all wet ingredients, except eggs, together in a bowl and mix thoroughly.
3. In another bowl, mix dry ingredients.
4. Gradually combine both bowls together and pour into cupcake tin.
5. Gradually beat eggs into the mixture, one egg at a time.
6. Bake for 15-20 minutes.

Matcha Cupcakes

Prep Time: 45 minutes
Servings: 12
Ingredients:
1/2 cup unsalted butter, softened
1 1/4 cups white sugar
2 eggs
1/2 cup milk
1/2 teaspoon vanilla extract
2 1/2 cups flour
2 tablespoons green tea powder

Directions:
1. Set oven to 350 degrees.
2. Combine all wet ingredients, except eggs, together in a bowl and mix thoroughly.
3. In another bowl, mix dry ingredients.
4. Gradually combine both bowls together and pour into cupcake tin.

5. Gradually beat eggs into the mixture, one egg at a time.
6. Bake for 15-20 minutes.

Vanilla Coconut Frosting

Prep Time: 10 minutes
Servings: 12
Ingredients:
1/4 cup butter, softened
4 ounces cream cheese, softened
1 cup confectioners' sugar
1/2 teaspoon vanilla extract
1/4 cup shredded coconut, or to taste

Directions:
1. Beat all ingredients together, except vanilla extract and lemon zest, until stiff peaks form.
2. Once smooth, add in remaining ingredients and mix until well incorporated.

Lemon Cream Frosting

Prep Time: 10 minutes
Servings: 12
Ingredients:
2 cups chilled heavy cream
3/4 cup confectioners' sugar
1 1/2 tablespoons fresh lemon juice

Directions:
1. Combine cream and lemon juice using an electric mixer on low.

2. Gradually add confectioner's sugar and beat until peaks form on high.

Vanilla Cream Cheese Frosting

Prep Time: 45 minutes
Servings: 12
Ingredients:
1 (8 ounce) package cream cheese, softened
1/4 cup butter, softened
2 tablespoons sour cream
2 teaspoons vanilla extract
1 box confectioners' sugar

Directions:
1. Combine all ingredients together in a bowl.
2. Beat on low using an electric mixer until smooth and thick.

Caramel Cream Frosting

Prep Time: 15 minutes
Servings: 12
Ingredients:
1/2 cup brown sugar
1/2 cup margarine
2 tablespoons light corn syrup
1 tablespoon vanilla extract
1/2 cup heavy cream, or as needed
1 pinch salt
3/4 cup salted butter, softened
2 cups confectioners' sugar, sifted

Directions:

1. In a saucepan, mix brown sugar, margarine, corn syrup and vanilla over medium heat.
2. Allow mixture to simmer until thick. Remove from heat and add cream gradually until you achieve a thick, syrupy consistency.
3. Season with salt and allow to cool.
4. Slowly beat confectioners' sugar and butter, using an electric mixer. Pour in caramel slowly—a tablespoon at a time—and mix until smooth.

Peanut Butter Frosting

Prep Time: 25 minutes
Servings: 12
Ingredients:
1 (12 ounce) tub pre-made vanilla frosting
3/4 cup creamy peanut butter

Directions:
1. Combine both ingredients using an electric mixer.

Chocolate Frosting

Prep Time: 10 minutes
Servings: 12
Ingredients:
1 (8 ounce) package cream cheese, softened
1 egg
1/3 cup white sugar
1/8 teaspoon salt
1 cup miniature semisweet chocolate chips

Directions:
1. Combine all ingredients except chocolate chips using an electric mixer.
2. Stir in chocolate chips.

PART 2

Introduction

Why are cupcakes so popular? If you have kids, you already know the answer.

They are small, perfectly equal, pre-sized cake dessert that takes no cutting or processing, are easily transportable, and can be eaten with the hands (no utensils required). Cupcakes have all the benefits of a regular cake with much less of the mess, or processing and handling worries. Also they are less intimidating for the beginner baker than a full blown cake.

Cupcakes are essentially small versions of a regular size cake, in most cases without a crust. If you plan on creating mini cakes without a cupcake liner, then a crust will most likely be required to keep the mini cake together.

You can basically use any cake recipe to make cupcakes thereby creating mini versions of your favorite cakes. That being said, there are slight differences, primarily with the baking time, that you need to consider with cupcakes. Also, you can take any of these cupcake recipes and create a full cake version with again primarily extending the baking time and adding for a crust.

If you have a favorite cake recipe that you would like to make cupcakes from I would recommend reading through the tips and best practices noted below. As for baking time, as a general rule, cut the full cake baking time $1/3^{rd}$ to determine how long to bake a cupcake version and look for the signs of doness.

Now, as for the recipes in this book, they are once again a collection of my favorites over time. As always, I have done the research, comparison analysis and more to get the best results. These recipes represent that work.

I strongly recommend reading through all the tips before starting any recipe. Also, before starting a recipe, read through the entire recipe closely, ingredients and directions. Don't make assumptions based on using any of my other recipes or even your own experience. On the other hand, I do welcome you to make any adjustments you feel will produce better results.

Tips & Best Practices

Utensils, Pans and other Equipment Requirements

- Electric mixer with a paddle attachment
- Mixing bowl
- Measuring cup and spoons
- Cupcake or muffin baking pan or tin with cups for 12 cupcakes
- Cupcake liners
- Pastry Bag. Create a homemade one by cutting a small hole in the corner of a zip lock bag
- Rubber Spatula
- Oven

General Tips

- Decide whether you want to make the standard cupcakes (i.e. with a cupcake liner that will be eaten by hand), or you want to use a favorite cake recipe and include the crust to create mini cake versions.
- Bring all refrigerated ingredients to room temperature prior to mixing, which includes eggs, butter, cream cheese, cream etc. This allows for more complete mixing and avoiding lumps.
- Using an electric mixer with a paddle attachment is recommended. Blend most ingredients at slow to medium speeds, using slow speed whenever adding sugar or other powdered ingredients.

- Generally blend one ingredient at a time. Don't add the next ingredient until the previous one has been blended into the mix. This includes adding one egg at a time.

- If flour, baking soda or cocoa powder is called for, it's best to sift these ingredients before adding them to this mix to minimize lumps in your batter.

- Stop beating at least twice while adding ingredients to scrape down the sides and blade with a rubber spatula.

- Combine butter and sugar, first on light speed then on medium until mixture is light and fluffy, which will require a little longer beating time after the ingredients are well combined. The butter will be lighter in color as air is added to the batter.

- Prior to lining your muffin or cupcake tin with the cupcake liners, spray a light coat of nonstick spray over the top surface. If your cupcakes bake and rise over onto the pan surface, the oily surface will keep them from sticking.

- The best tool for scooping and evenly distributing the batter mixture into the cupcake tin is a spring release ice cream scoop. Whatever tool you use to scoop out the batter, try to distribute the batter evenly among the cupcake cups.

- If you plan on making multiple pans of cupcakes, you need to place all the cupcakes into the one or multiple pre-heated ovens as soon as you are done distributing the batter. You don't want the raw batter to be sitting at room temperature because it will lose its leavening capacity (the ability of the dough to rise and expand)

Frosting / Icing Tips

- Cupcakes must cool down to room temperature before spreading frosting

- For a quick, more decorative and less messy means of spreading a thicker layer of frosting, use a pastry bag. If you don't have a pastry bag, scoop the frosting in a Ziploc bag (fill it up halfway only), squeeze out the air and close the seal. Cut a small hole on the corner of the bag. This will allow you to pile the frosting to heights you couldn't do with a spreading knife. If you do plan on creating a tall pile, multiply the frosting recipe ingredients by 1½ times to make sure you will have enough.

- Another option for a glazed type of topping is to dip or dunk the top edge of the cupcakes in a ganache (heated cream mixed with chocolate) or other more liquid cream mixture, twisting the cupcake as you lift it out to give it a slight twirl look.

Signs of Doneness

Start checking for signs of doneness just after 15 minutes. Most recipes call for a baking time of approximately 15 minutes but some ovens may run hotter so look for the following signs indicating your cupcakes are ready to remove from the oven:

Lightly touch the center with the tip of your finger. If the cupcake springs back then next stick a toothpick in the center and hold just for a second before pulling out. If there is any moist or wet batter on the toothpick, allow the cupcakes to bake for 2-3 more minutes. If the toothpick appears dry or clean or with crumbs attached, then your cupcakes are done.

Cooling Tips

Remove your cupcake pan(s) from the oven as soon as you see the signs of doneness and let them sit at room temperature for 10-15 minutes or until cool enough to handle. Remove the cupcakes from the pan and place them on a rack again at room temperature to completely cool to room temperature (another 15-20 minutes) before decorating or adding frosting.

Carrot Cake Cupcakes

Preparation Time:................**30 min**
Baking Time:........................**20 min**
Cooling Time:.......................**25 min**
Total – Ready to Serve In:.......1 hr 20 min
Number of Cupcakes: 12

Ingredients

Batter:

- 1 ½ cups all-purpose flour
- 1 ¼ teaspoons baking soda
- ½ teaspoon salt
- 1 ½ teaspoons ground cinnamon
- ½ teaspoon ground nutmeg
- ¼ teaspoon ground ginger
- 1 1/8 cups white sugar
- 1/3 cup brown sugar
- 2 eggs
- 1 teaspoon vanilla extract
- ½ cup vegetable oil
- 2 cups shredded carrots
- ½ cup crushed pineapple
- 1 cup chopped walnuts (optional)

Topping:

- 2 ounces white chocolate chips
- 1 small (4 ounce) package cream cheese, softened (cut an 8oz pack in half if unable to find the smaller packets)
- ¼ cup unsalted butter, softened

- 1 teaspoon vanilla extract
- ½ teaspoon orange extract
- 1 ½ cups confectioners' sugar
- 1 tablespoon heavy cream

Directions
1. Preheat oven to 350 degrees F (175 degrees C). Pull out your electric mixer using your paddle attachment. Lightly spray surface of cupcake pan with non-stick cooking spray. Line cupcake pans with 12 cupcake liners.
2. **Batter**: Mix flour, baking soda, salt, cinnamon, nutmeg and ginger. Set aside.
3. In a mixing bowl beat together on low speed white sugar, brown sugar and eggs. Add vanilla and oil and continue beating until well blended.
4. Using a rubber spatula, fold in carrots and pineapple into the egg and sugar mixture.
5. Slowly add in the flour mixture from Step 1 and beat on low speed until well blended.
6. Fold in walnuts and mix until evenly distributed.
7. Scoop the batter into the cupcake pan filling each cupcake ¾ full.
8. **Baking**: Bake at 350 degrees F for 20 minutes or until signs of doneness.
9. **Cooling**: Remove from oven and cool at room temperature for 10 minutes or until cool enough to handle. Remove cupcakes from pan and place on a rack at room temperature for another 15 minutes before spreading the frosting.
10. **Topping**: Heat white chocolate either in the top of a double boiler, or in a microwaveable bowl for 1 minute or so, until melted, in 15 second intervals. Stop the microwave every 15 seconds to stir the chocolate just until melted. Stir melted chocolate to cool to room temperature.
11. Beat together cream cheese and butter on medium speed until smooth.

12. Add melted white chocolate, vanilla and orange extract and continue to beat on low speed.
13. Gradually add in confectioners' sugar and beat on low. Add in heavy cream and beat until fluffy.
14. Spread on cupcakes using your pastry bag or zip lock bag and serve. Does not require refrigeration.

Cherry Cheesecake Cupcakes

Preparation Time:...............**25 min**
Baking Time:........................**25 min**
Cooling Time:......................**25 min**
Chilling Time:......................**2 hrs**
Total – Ready to Serve In:.......3 hrs 15 min
Number of Cupcakes: 24

Ingredients

Crust:
- 1 cup graham cracker crumbs
- 2 tablespoons white sugar
- 1/4 cup butter, melted

OR
- 24 vanilla wafer cookies (or substitute your favorite cookie)
        Batter:
- 3 (8 ounce) packages cream cheese (softened i.e. room temperature)
- 1 ¼ cups white sugar
- 1 tablespoon all-purpose flour
- 5 eggs
- 1 ½ teaspoons vanilla extract
- ¼ cup heavy whipping cream
- 1 tablespoon lemon juice
        Topping:

92

- 1 can of cherry pie filling

Directions
1. Preheat oven to 325 degrees F (165 degrees C). Pull out your electric mixer using your paddle attachment. Lightly spray surface of cupcake pan with non-stick cooking spray. Line cupcake pans with 24 cupcake liners.
2. **Crust option 1:** Mix graham cracker crumbs, white sugar and melted butter together until evenly moistened. Spread 1 tablespoon of crust mixture into each cupcake liner and lightly press crust mixture using the bottom of a small drinking glass.
3. **Crust option 2:** Place 1 vanilla wafer, flat side down, on the bottom or each cupcake liner
4. **Batter:** Beat softened cream cheese, sugar and flour together and beat on low until sugar and flour are mixed in. Turn mixer to medium speed and add one egg at a time to the mixture, letting each egg completely blend before adding the next one. Add vanilla with last egg. Add heavy cream and lemon juice and continue beating until all ingredients are blended and batter is creamy. Stop mixer at least twice during the adding of these ingredients and scrape down the sides and blade with a rubber spatula.
5. Scoop batter evenly over crust into paper lined cupcake pans filling each, leaving about ¼ to ½ inch on the top. They will expand some while cooking but will fall back after cooling.
6. **Baking:** Bake at 325 degrees F for 25 minutes or until signs of doneness.
7. **Cooling:** Remove from oven and cool at room temperature for 10 minutes or until cool enough to handle. Remove cupcakes from pan and place on a rack at room temperature for another 15 minutes before chilling.
8. Chilling: Refrigerate for at approximately 2 hours.
9. **Topping:** Add a spoon full of cherry pie filling and serve.

Chocolate Chip Cookie Dough Cupcakes

Preparation Time:...............**30 min**
Baking Time:.......................**18 min**
Cooling Time:......................**25 min**
Freezing Time:.....................**2 hrs**:
Total – Ready to Serve In:.......3 hr 13 min
Number of Cupcakes: 24

Ingredients

Batter:
Chocolate Chip Cookie Dough (Need to freeze before adding to cupcakes. To save time and effort, you can purchase premade frozen cookie dough or start from scratch using these ingredients)
- 1 teaspoon hot water
- ¼ teaspoon baking soda
- ½ cup butter, softened
- ¼ cup white sugar
- ½ cup brown sugar
- 1 egg
- 2 tablespoons whole milk
- 2 teaspoons vanilla extract
- ¼ teaspoon salt
- 1 ½ cups all-purpose flour
- 1 cup miniature semisweet chocolate chips

    Yellow Cake Batter
- 3 eggs
- 1 1/3 cups water
- 1/3 cup canola oil
- 1 (18.25 ounce) package yellow cake mix

Topping:

- Optional. Very good without or a good one is a light cream frosting to contrast with the chocolate chip cookie.

Directions

Chocolate Chip Cookie Dough – steps 1-4 (if premade from the store skip to step 4)
1. Heat up 2 teaspoons of water in microwave and add baking soda. Stir and dissolve baking soda. Set aside.
2. Spray a non-stick cooking spray or lightly oil a baking sheet that can fit in your freezer.
3. Pull out your electric mixer using your paddle attachment. Beat butter, white sugar, and brown sugar together on low speed until all sugar is blended. Add one whole egg and to this mixture. Slowly mix in milk, vanilla, salt, baking soda solution, flour and finally chocolate chips until evenly distributed.
4. Using a small spoon, scoop out and form the dough into small tablespoon sized balls and place the balls onto your non-stick cookie sheet. Freeze the balls for approximately 2 hours or until they are completely frozen.
   ****Two Hours Later****
5. Preheat oven to 350 degrees F (175 degrees C). Pull out your electric mixer using your paddle attachment. Lightly spray surface of cupcake pan with non-stick cooking spray. Line cupcake pans with 24 cupcake liners.
6. **Batter**: Add 3 eggs to mixing bowl and beat on low just enough to blend together.
7. Add water, canola oil and slowly add cake mix to egg mixture. Turn speed up to medium and beat for approximately 2 minutes.
8. Scoop the batter into the cupcake pan filling each cupcake 2/3 full.
9. Place a frozen cookie dough ball (do not defrost dough) into the top and center of the batter of each cupcake.

10. **Baking:** Bake at 350 degrees F for 18 minutes or until signs of doneness - stick a toothpick into the outside cake layer (not into the cookie dough) after about 16 minutes. If toothpick comes out clean, remove cupcakes from the oven.
11. **Cooling:** Remove from oven and cool at room temperature for 10 minutes or until cool enough to handle. Remove cupcakes from pan and place on a rack at room temperature for another 15 minutes before spreading the frosting.
12. **Topping:** Optional. Very good without, but also very good with a light butter cream or vanilla cream frosting to contrast with the chocolate chip cookie dough. Does not require refrigeration.

Chocolate Cinnamon Cupcakes

Preparation Time:…………..**20 min**
Baking Time:…………………..**15 min**
Cooling Time:…………………**25 min**
Total – Ready to Serve In:…1 hr
Number of Cupcakes: 24

Ingredients

Batter:

- 1 ½ cups all-purpose flour
- 1 cup white sugar
- 1 teaspoon baking powder
- 1/3 cup unsweetened cocoa powder
- ½ teaspoon salt
- ¾ cup milk
- ½ cup butter, melted

- 3 eggs
- 1 teaspoon ground cinnamon
- 1 teaspoon vanilla extract

Topping:

- ½ cup butter
- ½ cup butter-flavored shortening
- 1 pinch salt
- 1 tablespoon ground cinnamon
- 1 tablespoon unsweetened cocoa powder
- 1 teaspoon vanilla extract
- 3 cups confectioners' (powdered) sugar
- ¼ cup milk
- 1 cup confectioners' (powdered) sugar

Directions
1. Preheat oven to 350 degrees F (175 degrees C). Pull out your electric mixer using your paddle attachment. Lightly spray surface of cupcake pan with non-stick cooking spray. Line cupcake pans with 24 cupcake liners.
2. **Batter:** Mix together flour, sugar, baking powder, cocoa and salt. Set aside.
3. Beat milk, melted butter on low speed until mixed together. Add one egg at a time to this mixture, letting each egg completely blend before adding the next one. Mix in cinnamon, and vanilla.
4. Slowly add flour, cocoa dry mixture from step 2. Turn speed up to medium and beat for 2 more minutes. Stop mixture twice to scrap down the sides and the paddle with a rubber spatula.
5. Scoop the batter into the cupcake pans filling each cupcake 2/3 full.
6. **Baking:** Bake at 350 degrees F for 15 minutes or until see signs of doneness.

7. **Cooling:** Remove from oven and cool at room temperature for 10 minutes or until cool enough to handle. Remove cupcakes from pan and place on a rack at room temperature for another 15 minutes before spreading the frosting.

8. **Frosting:** While cupcakes are cooling, mix together ½ cup butter and ½ cup butter flavored shortening in your mixing bowl on low speed until smooth. Mix in salt, 1 tablespoon cinnamon, 1 tablespoon cocoa powder, 1 teaspoon vanilla3 cups confectioners' sugar and ¼ cup milk. Lastly, add in 1 additional cup of confectioners' sugar and beat until completely mixed together and frosting is light enough to easily spread with a knife or small spatula. Or use a zip lock bag with a hole cut out of the corner.

9. **Topping:** Spread on cupcakes using your pastry bag or zip lock bag and serve. Does not require refrigeration.

Chocolate Raspberry Cheesecake Cupcakes

Preparation Time:..............**30 min**
Baking Time:......................**20 min**
Cooling Time:.....................**25 min**
Total – Ready to Serve In:...1 hr 5 min
Number of Cupcakes: 18-24

Ingredients

Filling Layer 1:

- 1 ½ cups all-purpose flour
- 1 cup white sugar
- ¼ cup unsweetened cocoa powder
- 1 teaspoon baking soda
- ½ teaspoon salt
- 1 cup milk

- 1/3 cup vegetable oil
- 1 tablespoon cider vinegar
- 1 teaspoon vanilla extract

Filling Layer 2: (mixed first)

- 1 (8 ounce) package cream cheese, softened
- 1 egg
- 1/3 cup white sugar
- 1/8 teaspoon salt
- 1 cup miniature semisweet chocolate chips
  Topping

- 1 jar raspberry preserves

Directions
1. Preheat oven to 350 degrees F (175 degrees C). Pull out your electric mixer using your paddle attachment. Lightly spray surface of cupcake pan with non-stick cooking spray. Line cupcake pans with 24 cupcake liners.
2. **Filling Layer 2**: Combine and beat on low speed the cream cheese, 1 egg, 1/3 cup sugar and 1/8 teaspoon salt until just blended together and no longer lumpy. Don't over beat. Hand mix in the chocolate chips. Set aside.
3. **Filling Layer 1**: In a large bowl, hand stir together flour, 1 cup of sugar, cocoa, baking soda and ½ teaspoon salt. After combined, make a well in the center of the dry mixture and add in the milk, oil, vinegar and vanilla. Mix until completely blended together.
4. Scoop Layer 1 batter into the paper lined cupcake pans filling each cupcake to only about 1/3 full. Scoop a small to medium spoon full of the Layer 2 cream cheese mixture on top of the layer 1 batter. Evenly distribute the cheesecake mixture over the cupcakes.

5. **Baking:** Bake at 350 degrees F for 20 minutes or until signs of doneness.
6. **Cooling:** Remove from oven and cool at room temperature for 10 minutes or until cool enough to handle. Remove cupcakes from pan and place on a rack at room temperature for another 15 minutes before spreading the preserves.
7. **Topping:** Lightly warm the raspberry preserves in a sauce pan or the microwave to make it easier to spread on the cupcakes. Does not require refrigeration.

Lemon Cream Cupcakes

Preparation Time:............**25 min**
Baking Time:.....................**15 min**
Cooling Time:....................**25 min**
Total – Ready to Serve In:...1 hr 5 min
Number of Cupcakes: 30

Ingredients

Batter:

- 3 cups all-purpose flour
- 3 teaspoons baking powder
- ½ teaspoon salt
- 1 cup unsalted butter, softened (room temperature)
- 2 cups white sugar
- 4 eggs (warmed to room temperature)
- 1 teaspoon vanilla extract
- 2 tablespoons lemon zest
- 1 cup whole milk
- 2 ½ tablespoons fresh lemon juice
  Lemon Cream Icing

- 2 cups chilled heavy cream
- ¾ cup confectioners' sugar
- 1 ½ tablespoons fresh lemon juice

Directions

1. Preheat oven to 375 degrees F (190 degrees C). Pull out your electric mixer using your paddle attachment. Lightly spray surface of cupcake pan with non-stick cooking spray. Line cupcake pans with 30 cupcake liners.
2. **Batter**: Mix flour, baking powder and salt together. Set aside.
3. Beat butter and sugar together on low speed until fluffy.
4. Add one egg at a time to butter sugar mixture, letting each egg completely blend before adding the next one. Add vanilla and lemon zest and beat until blended together
5. Slowly add in ½ of flour mixture, then add ½ of the milk (½ cup) and ½ of the lemon juice (1 ¼ lemon juice) . Let blend together and repeat again adding remaining flour, milk and lemon juice. Beat on low until just blended together. Do not overbeat.
6. Scoop the batter into the cupcake pans filling each cupcake ¾ full.
7. **Baking:** Bake at 375 degrees F for 15 minutes or until signs of doneness.
8. **Cooling:** Remove from oven and cool at room temperature for 10 minutes or until cool enough to handle. Remove cupcakes from pan and place on a rack at room temperature for another 15 minutes before spreading the frosting.
9. **Topping/Icing:** Beat chilled heavy cream on low until cream begins to thicken. Slowly add confectioners' sugar and lemon juice and continue beating until fully blended.
10. Turn speed to high and continue beating until icing from soft peaks (about 5 minutes).

11. Spread on cupcakes using your pastry bag or zip lock bag and serve. Refrigerate leftovers.

Red Velvet Cupcakes

Preparation Time:.............**25 min**
Baking Time:.....................**18 min**
Cooling Time:....................**25 min**
Total – Ready to Serve In:...1 hr 8 min
Number of Cupcakes: 30

Ingredients

Batter:
- 2 cups all-purpose flour
- ½ cup unsweetened cocoa powder
- 1 teaspoon baking soda
- ½ teaspoon salt
- 1 cup butter, softened
- 2 ¼ cups sugar
- 4 eggs
- 1 cup sour cream
- ½ cup milk
- 1 (1 ounce) bottle red food coloring (yes ... one whole 1 ounce bottle)
- 3 teaspoons vanilla extract
    Topping: **(Vanilla Cream Cheese Frosting)**
- 1 (8 ounce) package cream cheese, softened
- ¼ cup butter, softened
- 2 tablespoons sour cream
- 2 teaspoons vanilla extract

- 1 (16 ounce) box confectioners' (powdered) sugar

Directions
1. Preheat oven to 350 degrees F (175 degrees C). Pull out your electric mixer using your paddle attachment. Lightly spray surface of cupcake pan with non-stick cooking spray. Line cupcake pans with 30 cupcake liners.
2. **Batter**: Mix flour, cocoa powder, baking soda and salt in medium bowl. Set aside.
3. Beat butter and sugar in large bowl with electric mixer initially on low speed then once sugar is partially blended turn up to medium speed and beat for five minutes or until light and fluffy. Add one egg at a time, letting each egg completely blend before adding the next one. Add sour cream, milk, red food coloring and vanilla. Slowly beat in flour mixture from step 2 on low speed just until mixture is blended in. Do not overbeat.
4. Scoop batter into paper lined cupcake pans filling each cupcake 2/3 full.
5. **Baking:** Bake at 350 degrees F for 18 minutes or until signs of doneness.
6. **Cooling:** Remove from oven and cool at room temperature for 10 minutes or until cool enough to handle. Remove cupcakes from pan and place on a rack at room temperature for another 15 minutes before spreading the frosting.
7. **Topping:** While cupcakes are cooling, beat together on slow speed, softened cream cheese, butter, sour cream and vanilla until light and fluffy. Slowly add in powdered sugar until mixture is completely blended and smooth
8. Spread on cupcakes using your pastry bag or zip lock bag and serve. Does not require refrigeration.

The Chocolate Cupcake

Preparation Time:...............**25 min**
Baking Time:.......................**15 min**

Cooling Time:..........................**25 min**
Total – Ready to Serve In:...1 hr 5 min
Number of Cupcakes: 24

Ingredients

Batter:
- 2 cups all-purpose flour
- 2 cups sugar
- ½ teaspoon baking powder
- 1 teaspoon salt
- 1 teaspoon baking soda
- ½ cup shortening (hydrogenated vegetable oil, or butter softened - room temperature,if preferred)
- ¾ cup milk
- ¾ cup water
- 2 large eggs
- 1 teaspoon vanilla extract
- 4 ounces melted unsweetened baking chocolate (unsweetened or bitter chocolate)

Topping:

- Any popular chocolate cake frosting. For a rich homemade version, see my recipe under the Vanilla Cream Filled Double Chocolate Cupcakes below.

Directions
1. Preheat oven to 350 degrees F (175 degrees C). Pull out your electric mixer using your paddle attachment. Lightly spray surface of cupcake pan with non-stick cooking spray. Line cupcake pans with 24 cupcake liners.
2. **Batter**: Mix together flour, sugar, baking powder, salt and baking soda with a large spoon. Add in shortening, milk and water and beat on low speed until mixed together. Add one egg at a time to this mixture, letting each egg completely

104

blend before adding the next one. Add vanilla. Turn speed to medium and beat for 3 more minutes. Stop mixture twice to scrap down the sides and the paddle with a rubber spatula.

3. While batter is mixing, break up chocolate and melt either in a double boiler, or in a microwaveable bowl for 1 to 2 minutes or until melted, in 10 to 15 second intervals. Stop the microwave every 10 to 15 seconds to stir the chocolate just until melted.

4. Add melted chocolate to batter and continue beating on medium speed until chocolate is blended in.

5. Scoop the batter into the cupcake pans filling each cupcake 2/3 full.

6. **Baking:** Bake at 350 degrees F for 15 minutes or until signs of doneness.

7. **Cooling:** Remove from oven and cool at room temperature for 10 minutes or until cool enough to handle. Remove cupcakes from pan and place on a rack at room temperature for another 15 minutes before spreading the frosting.

8. **Topping:** Spread on cupcakes using your pastry bag or zip lock bag and serve. Does not require refrigeration.

Triple Chocolate Cream Filled Cupcakes

Preparation Time:............**45 min**
Baking Time:.....................**15 min**
Cooling Time:.....................**25 min**
Total – Ready to Serve In:...1 hr 25 min
Number of Cupcakes: 24

Ingredients

Batter:
• 3 cups all-purpose flour

- 1 teaspoon baking soda
- ¼ teaspoon salt
- ¾ cup hot water
- ¾ cup unsweetened cocoa powder
- 1 ½ cups unsalted butter (3 sticks)
- 2 ¼ cups white sugar
- 4 large eggs, at room temperature
- 3 teaspoons vanilla extract
- 1 cup sour cream, at room temperature

Filling:
- 4 tablespoons unsalted butter, at room temperature
- 1 cup heavy cream
- 8 oz. bittersweet chocolate, finely chopped

Topping – rich chocolate frosting (feel free to use a favorite store purchased chocolate cake frosting for faster turnaround):

- 1 (8 oz) package of cream cheese softened (room temperature)
- 9 tablespoons unsalted butter, at room temperature
- 3 cups confectioners' sugar, sifted to remove lumps
- 6 tablespoons unsweetened cocoa powder
- 1/16 teaspoon salt (a pinch)
- 14 oz. bittersweet chocolate, finely chopped
- 1 cup sour cream

Directions
1. Preheat oven to 350 degrees F (175 degrees C). Pull out your electric mixer using your paddle attachment. Lightly spray surface of cupcake pan with non-stick cooking spray. Line cupcake pans with 24 cupcake liners.
2. **Batter:** Mix flour, baking soda and salt in medium bowl. Set aside.
3. In a small bowl, combine hot water and cocoa and whisk together until smooth. Set aside.

106

4. Cut butter into 4-5 chunks and add with sugar to a medium sauce pan over medium heat. Heat and mix together until butter is melted. Remove from heat and pour into your mixing bowl.
5. Beat butter sugar mixture on low speed for 4 minutes or until cooled.
6. Add one egg at a time to the mixture, letting each egg completely blend before adding the next one. Add vanilla with last egg. Add sour cream and then cocoa mixture from step 3. Stop mixing twice and scrape down the sides with a rubber spatula. Beat until well blended.
7. Slowly add in dry ingredient mixture, beating until well blended.
8. Scoop the batter into the cupcake pans filling each cupcake about ¾ full.
9. **Baking:** Bake at 350 degrees F for 15 minutes or until signs of doneness.
10. **Cooling:** Remove from oven and cool at room temperature for 10 minutes or until cool enough to handle. Leave cupcakes in baking pan (easier to add cream filling). Do not fill with filling (next step) until completely cool.
11. **Chocolate Filling:** In your mixing bowl, beat butter and cream on low speed until smooth and blended.
12. Heat chopped chocolate either in the top of a double boiler, or in a microwaveable bowl for 1 minute or so, until melted, in 15 second intervals. Stop the microwave every 15 seconds to stir the chocolate just until melted. Overheating with scorch the chocolate. Stir melted chocolate to cool to just warm before adding to butter cream mixer.
13. Beat in melted chocolate until blended.
14. Use a small knife to cut out a small cone shape from the middle of the cupcake, or use an apple corer to cut out a round plug. Save the plugs on the side. To fill cupcakes there are a few option:

- If you have one, fill a pastry bag with chocolate filling and fill each cupcake leaving enough room to cap off with cap from the plug just cut out (fill about 2/3rds full)
- Or create a homemade pastry bag by filling a zip lock back with the chocolate filling, seal the bag and cut one small corner of the bag and squeeze out the filling into each cupcake to about 2/3rds full.

Cut the bottom of the plugs you just created into smaller caps and replace onto the top on the chocolate filled center.

Topping: Beat cream cheese and butter on medium speed until blended together and fluffy – about 3 minutes. Slowly add the confectioners' sugar, cocoa powder and salt. Beat until well blended.

Heat chopped chocolate either in the top of a double boiler, or in a microwaveable bowl for 1 minute or so, until melted, in 15 second intervals. Stop the microwave every 15 seconds to stir the chocolate just until melted. Overheating with scorch the chocolate. Stir melted chocolate to cool to just warm before adding to cream cheese mixture.

Beat in the melted chocolate and then add sour cream to the cream cheese mixture.

Spread on cupcakes using your pastry bag or zip lock bag and serve. Does not require refrigeration.

Vanilla Cream Filled Double Chocolate Cupcakes

Preparation Time:.............**45 min**
Baking Time:......................**15 min**
Cooling Time:....................**25 min**
Total – Ready to Serve In:...1 hr 25 min
Number of Cupcakes: 36

Ingredients

Batter:

- 3 cups all-purpose flour
- 2 cups white sugar
- 1/3 cup unsweetened cocoa powder
- 2 teaspoons baking soda
- 1 teaspoon salt
- 1 cup milk
- 1 cup water
- 1 cup vegetable oil
- 1 teaspoon vanilla extract
- 2 eggs
  Filling:

- ¼ cup butter
- ¼ cup shortening
- 2 cups confectioners' (powdered) sugar
- ½ teaspoon salt
- 3 tablespoons milk
- 1 teaspoon vanilla extract

Topping – rich chocolate frosting (feel free to use a favorite store-purchased chocolate cake frosting for faster turnaround):

- ½ cup butter, room temperature
- 1/3 cup whipping cream
- 1/8 teaspoon salt (a pinch)
- ½ cup unsweetened cocoa powder
- 1 teaspoon vanilla extract
- 3 ½ cups confectioners' sugar, sifted to remove lumps

Directions

1. Preheat oven to 375 degrees F (190 degrees C). Pull out your electric mixer using your paddle attachment. Lightly spray surface of cupcake pan with non-stick cooking spray. Line cupcake pans with 36 cupcake liners.
2. **Batter**: Mix flour, sugar, cocoa powder, baking soda and salt in medium bowl. Set aside.
3. Beat milk, water, oil and vanilla together on low speed. Add one egg at a time, letting each egg completely blend before adding the next one. Slowly beat in flour and cocoa mixture from step 2 on low speed until mixture is well blended. Do not overbeat.
4. Scoop the batter into the cupcake pans filling each cupcake 2/3 full.
5. **Baking:** Bake at 375 degrees F for 15 minutes or until signs of doneness.
6. **Cooling:** Remove from oven and cool at room temperature for 25 minutes or until cool enough to handle. Leave cupcakes in baking pan (easier to add cream filling). Do not fill with cream filling (next step) until completely cool.
7. **Cream Filling:** In your mixing bowl, beat butter and shortening on low speed until smooth and blended. Add confectioners' sugar and salt and slowly add in 3 tablespoons of milk and 1 teaspoon vanilla. Beat until cream mixture is light and fluffy.
8. Use a small knife to cut out a small cone shape from the middle of the cupcake, or use an apple corer to cut out a round plug. Save the plugs on the side. To fill cupcakes there are a few options:
- If you have one, fill a pastry bag with cream filling and fill each cupcake leaving enough room to cap off with cap from the plug just cut out (fill about 2/3rds full)
- Or create a homemade pastry bag by filling a zip lock back with the cream filling, seal the bag and cut one small corner of the bag and squeeze out the filling into each cupcake to about 2/3rds full.

Cut the bottom of the plugs you just created into smaller caps and replace onto the top on the cream filled center.

Topping: Beat butter, cream and salt on low to medium speed until blended together. Turn to low speed and slowly add the cocoa powder and beat until creamy. Add vanilla and then slowly add confectioners' sugar. Turn speed to medium and beat for about 5 minutes until creamy and fluffy. Frosting will set up firm so spread on cupcakes right away.

Spread on cupcakes using your pastry bag or zip lock bag and serve. Does not require refrigeration.

CUPCAKES Recipes

Chocolate Lovers Delight

Servings: 12

Ingredients:
1½ cups cake flour
¼ cup cocoa
½ teaspoon baking soda
1 teaspoon baking powder
½ teaspoon salt
½ cup fat free milk
¾ cup sweeteners
4 egg whites
2/3 cup fat-free plain yogurt
1 teaspoon vanilla extract

Preparation:

Place the oven on to a temperature of 200 Degrees Celsius. In a bowl, mix together all of the wet ingredients. In another bowl, mix together all of the dry ingredients. Combine them slowly using a wooden spoon.
Either use a greased muffin tin or a muffin tin with cupcake holder and fill them up to 3/4's full. Bake for 15 to 20 minutes or until a toothpick or skewer pole into the middle comes out clean.

Vanilla Cupcakes

Servings: 12

Ingredients:

2 cups cake flour

1 egg

2 egg whites

1 cup sweeteners

1 teaspoon baking powder

½ teaspoon baking soda

½ teaspoon salt

1 teaspoon vanilla extract

½ cup fat free milk
¼ cup vegetable oil
¼ cup fat-free plain yogurt

Preparation:

Place the oven on to a temperature of 180 Degrees Celsius. In a bowl, mix together all of the wet ingredients. In another bowl, mix together all of the dry ingredients. Combine them slowly using a wooden spoon.

Either use a greased muffin tin or a muffin tin with cupcake holder and fill them up to 3/4's full. Bake for 15 to 20 minutes or until a toothpick or skewer pole into the middle comes out clean.

Lemon Cupcakes

Servings: 12

Ingredients:

1¾ cups white flour

1 teaspoon baking soda

½ teaspoon baking powder

½ teaspoon salt

½ cup unsweetened applesauce

½ cup sweeteners

1 Tablespoon vegetable oil

1 egg

1 cup fat-free sour cream

½ lemon's juice

½ lemon's zest

Preparation:

Place the oven on to a temperature of 180 Degrees Celsius. In a bowl mix the dry ingredients. In another bowl, mix together the applesauce, oil and the sugar using a whisk or an electric beater. Then add the egg and beat together well. When mixed, stir in the lemon and the zest using a wooden spoon.

Once mixed, add the sour cream and the flour alternatively, stirring between each addition.

Either use a greased muffin tin or a muffin tin with cupcake holder and fill them up to 3/4's full. Bake for 20 to 25 minutes or until a toothpick or skewer pole into the middle comes out clean.

Red Velvet Cupcakes

Servings: 12

Ingredients:
1 ¾ cups cake flour
¼ cup cocoa
1 cup sweetener
½ cup unsweetened applesauce
¼ cup vegetable oil
¾ cup fat-free egg substitute
2 Tablespoons red food colouring

1 teaspoon vanilla extract
½ cup fat-free buttermilk
1¼ teaspoon white vinegar
½ teaspoon salt
1 teaspoon baking soda

Preparation:

Place the oven on to a temperature of 180 Degrees Celsius.
In a bowl, mix together the flour, salt and cocoa until combined.
In another bowl, mix the applesauce and sugar with a whisk and
then add in the egg substitute. Add in the food colouring and the
vanilla as well as the buttermilk. Once mixed, add in the flour in
small portions whilst stirring between each addition. In a small
bowl, mix the vinegar and the baking powder so that it becomes
fizzy and then fold this into the mixture.
Either use a greased muffin tin or a muffin tin with cupcake
holder and fill them up to 3/4's full. Bake for 15 to 20 minutes or
until a toothpick or skewer pole into the middle comes out
clean.

Blueberry Potato Cupcakes

Servings: 12

Ingredients:

1 large potato, peeled and cut into cubes
11/2 cup flour
1½ teaspoons baking powder
½ teaspoon baking soda
½ teaspoon salt
¾ cup sweeteners
¼ cup vegetable oil
1 large egg
½ teaspoon vanilla extract
½ cup fat free buttermilk
1 cup blueberries

Preparation:

Place the oven on to a temperature of 180 Degrees Celsius.
Boil the potato in a pot until soft. Then drain the water and
mash the potato up until it is smooth. Fill up ¾ 's of a cup and
leave it to cool. In a bowl, mix together the flour, baking powder,
½ a teaspoon of salt and the baking soda.
In a separate bowl, mix together the sweetener and oil until
smooth. Beat in the ½ a teaspoon of vanilla as well as the egg
and the ¾ cup of mashed potatoes. When combined, add in the
dry mixture with the buttermilk alternatively. Fold in a cup of
blueberries with a wooden spoon.
Either use a greased muffin tin or a muffin tin with cupcake
holder and fill them up. Bake for 22 to 24 minutes or until a
toothpick or skewer pole into the middle comes out clean.

Apple Cupcakes

Servings: 12
Ingredients:
1½ cups apples, peeled and grated
½ cup diced dried apples
3 tablespoons sweeteners
¾ cup sweeteners
1 teaspoon cinnamon
1/3 cup canola oil
2 large eggs
1 teaspoon vanilla extract
1½ cup cake flour
¾ teaspoon baking soda
¼ teaspoon salt
½ cup fat free buttermilk

Preparation:
Place the oven on to a temperature of 180 Degrees Celsius.
Mix together the grated apple along with the dried apple pieces
into a bowl containing the sugar and the cinnamon. Coat well. In
a separate bowl mix the oil and the cup of sweetener until they
are well combined. Beat in the eggs individually and then add
the vanilla extract whilst increasing the speed at which you are
beating the mixture.

In a separate bowl, mix the flour, baking soda and the salt together and then add the buttermilk and alternating with the dry ingredient mix. Stir in the apple mix.

Either use a greased muffin tin or a muffin tin with cupcake holder and fill them up. Bake for 20 to 22 minutes or until a toothpick or skewer pole into the middle comes out clean.

Confetti Cupcakes

Servings: 24

Ingredients:
1 packet of Pillsbury Funfetti Cake Mix
1 can Sprite Zero

Preparation:
Place the oven on to a temperature of 180 Degrees Celsius. In a bowl, mix together all of the ingredients until smooth. Either use a greased muffin tin or a muffin tin with cupcake holder and fill them up to 1/4 full.

Bake for 20 minutes or until a toothpick or skewer pole into the middle comes out clean.

Raspberry Smoothie Cupcakes

Servings: 12

Ingredients:

2 cups raspberries
12 fresh berries for garnish
1 tablespoon sweetener
¾ cup sweetener
11/2 cups flour
1 ½ teaspoons baking powder
½ teaspoon baking soda
½ teaspoon salt
¼ cup canola oil
2 large eggs
1 teaspoon vanilla extract
1 teaspoon freshly grated lemon zest
1/2 cup fat free buttermilk

Preparation:

Place the oven on to a temperature of 180 Degrees Celsius. In a blender, puree the 2 cups of raspberries and then place the pureed raspberries into a strainer to discard the seeds. (Keep 4 teaspoons if you are doing a raspberry frosting).
Mix together the flour, baking powder, salt and the baking soda until combined. In a separate bowl, mix the ¾ cup of sweetener and the oil and then beat in the eggs, vanilla extract and lemon zest until mixed together well. Then add the dry ingredients and the buttermilk alternatively.
Either use a greased muffin tin or a muffin tin with cupcake holder and fill them up to 3/4's full. If you have raspberry puree

spare, place a little on top of each cupcake. Bake for 22 to 24 minutes or until a toothpick or skewer pole into the middle comes out clean.

Berry Picking Cupcakes

Servings: 12
Ingredients:

1½ cups cake flour
½ cup cocoa
1½ teaspoons baking powder
1 teaspoon vanilla extract
½ cup fat free buttermilk
½ teaspoon baking soda
½ teaspoon salt
¾ cup sweetener
¼ cup canola oil
1 large egg
1½ cups chopped pitted cherries
12 cherries for garnish
You can use strawberries in place of the cherries.

Preparation:

Place the oven on to a temperature of 180 Degrees Celsius.

Mix together the flour, baking powder, salt and the baking soda until combined. In a separate bowl, mix the ¾ cup of sweetener and the oil and then beat in the eggs, vanilla extract until mixed together well. Then add the dry ingredients and the buttermilk alternatively and fold in the chopped cherries.

Either use a greased muffin tin or a muffin tin with cupcake holder and fill them up to 3/4's full. Bake for 22 to 26 minutes or until a toothpick or skewer pole into the middle comes out clean.

Vanilla Sinless Cupcakes

Servings: 10
Ingredients:
1 cup white flour

1 teaspoon baking powder

½ teaspoon salt
½ teaspoon baking soda
1 Tablespoon ground flaxseed
4 Tablespoon sweeteners
2 Tablespoons sweetener
1 Tablespoon vanilla extract
1 cup plain yogurt
¼ cup fat free milk
3 Tablespoon canola oil

Preparation:

Place the oven on to a temperature of 180 Degrees Celsius. In a bowl, mix together all of the wet ingredients with the flaxseed. In another bowl, mix together all of the dry ingredients. Combine them slowly using a wooden spoon.
Either use a greased muffin tin or a muffin tin with cupcake holder and fill them up to 3/4's full.
Bake for 18 to 20 minutes or until a toothpick or skewer pole into the middle comes out clean.

Angel Meringue Cupcakes

Servings: 12
Ingredients:

½ cup sweeteners

2/3 cup cake flour

¼ teaspoon salt

8 egg whites
¼ cup water
1 teaspoon vanilla extract

¼ teaspoon cream of tartar
½ cup sweeteners

Preparation:
Place the oven on to a temperature of 160 Degrees Celsius.
In a bowl, mix together the sweeteners, salt and the cake flour.
In another bowl, mix together the egg whites, water, cream of tartar and the vanilla. Mix this together well until it starts to foam and then slowly add the 2nd ½ cup of sweeteners in small intervals whilst mixing. Once all the sugar is in, mix on a high speed until the mixture forms peaks. Add the dry ingredients and fold them in carefully.
Either use a greased muffin tin or a muffin tin with cupcake holder and fill them up to 3/4's full.
Bake for 18 minutes or until the tops are a slight golden colour.

Citrus Fun Cupcakes

Servings: 30
Ingredients:
One box of vanilla cake mix
1 can of Diet orange pop

Preparation:
Place the oven on to a temperature of 180 Degrees Celsius.

Take the white cake mix and mix it together with the can of orange pop . Take a tablespoon dip the batter into the paper cupcakes pan and bake for 8 to 10 min. or until they are brown.
Either use a greased muffin tin or a muffin tin with cupcake holder and fill them up to ½ full.
Bake for 15 to 20 minutes or until a toothpick or skewer pole into the middle comes out clean.

Strawberry Cupcakes

Servings: 24
Ingredients:

1 box Pilsbury Moist Supreme, Strawberry flavour
1 can Sierra Mist Free

Preparation:
Place the oven on to a temperature of 180 Degrees Celsius. In a bowl, mix together the cake mix and the can of soda.
Either use a greased muffin tin or a muffin tin with cupcake holder and fill them up to 3/4's full.
Bake for 18 to 22 minutes or until a toothpick or skewer pole into the middle comes out clean.

Chocolate Coma Cupcakes

Servings: 12
Ingredients:

2 cup cake flour

1 teaspoon baking soda

1 large egg

1 large egg yolk

1 teaspoon vanilla extract

½ teaspoon salt

1 cup sweetener

¼ cup canola oil

1 vanilla pod

½ cup unsweetened applesauce

1 can low-fat evaporated milk

Preparation:

Place the oven on to a temperature of 180 Degrees Celsius.
In a bowl, mix together the flour, baking soda and salt. In another bowl, mix together the sweetener and oil. Scrape the vanilla paste out of the vanilla pod and add it into the mixture. Then add the egg, egg yolks, apple sauce and the vanilla extra and mix together well. Then add the dry ingredients slowly and alternatively with the milk.
Either use a greased muffin tin or a muffin tin with cupcake holder and fill them up to 3/4's full.
Bake for 20 to 22 minutes or until a toothpick or skewer pole into the middle comes out clean.

Peach Cupcakes

Servings: 12

Ingredients:

6 semi-ripe peaches

½ cup butter softened

1 cup sugar

2 large eggs

1 teaspoon vanilla

½ teaspoon baking soda

½ teaspoon baking powder

¼ teaspoon salt

1½ cup flour

½ cup fat free buttermilk

Preparation:
Place the oven on to a temperature of 200 Degrees Celsius. Peel and dice the peaches and then bake them for about 25 to 30 minutes in the oven.
Change the oven temperature to 180 Degrees Celsius.
Mix the dry ingredients together in a bowl. In a separate bowl, mix together the butter and sugar and beat it until it is smooth and white. Once this is done, add 1/3 of the dry ingredients and ½ the milk. Once combined, add the rest of the ingredients and then fold in roasted peaches.
Either use a greased muffin tin or a muffin tin with cupcake holder and fill them up to 3/4's full. Bake for 18 to 20 minutes or until a toothpick or skewer pole into the middle comes out clean.

Peanut Butter Chocolate Cupcakes

Servings: 12

Ingredients:
¾ cup sweeteners
¼ cup creamy peanut butter
¼ cup fat-free sour cream
1 egg
1 egg white
1 cup flour
¼ cup baking cocoa
½ cup hot water
½ teaspoon baking soda
1/3 cup semisweet chocolate chips

Preparation:
Place the oven on to a temperature of 180 Degrees Celsius.
In a bowl, mix together the sweetener, peanut butter, sour cream, egg and egg white until well blended. Beat in remaining ingredients except powdered sugar on low speed just until mixed.
Either use a greased muffin tin or a muffin tin with cupcake holder and fill them up to 3/4's full. Bake for 15 to 20 minutes or until a toothpick or skewer pole into the middle comes out clean.

Choccie Lottie Cupcakes

Servings: 12

Ingredients:

1 cup fat free milk

1 teaspoon apple cider vinegar

¾ cup sweetener

1/3 cup canola oil

11/2 teaspoon vanilla extract

1 cup flour

1/3 cup cocoa

¾ teaspoon baking soda

½ teaspoon baking powder

¼ teaspoon salt

Preparation:

Place the oven on to a temperature of 180 Degrees Celsius.
In a bowl, mix together milk and vinegar and allow it to curdle.
When curdled, add the sweetener, oil and vanilla and beat it
until it becomes a foam like substance. In another bowl, mix
together the flour, cocoa powder, baking soda, baking powder,
and salt. Mix into the wet mixture.
Either use a greased muffin tin or a muffin tin with cupcake
holder and fill them up to 3/4's full. Bake for 18 to 20 minutes or
until a toothpick or skewer pole into the middle comes out
clean.

Oreo Cupcakes

Servings: 24

Ingredients:

1 packet chocolate cake mix

1 packet Philadelphia cheese

1 egg

1 Tablespoon sweeteners

48 mini oreos

1 ½ cups cook whip topping

Preparation:

Place the oven on to a temperature of 180 Degrees Celsius.
In a bowl, mix together cream cheese, egg and sugar until well
blended. Either use a greased muffin tin or a muffin tin with
cupcake holder and fill them up to ½ full. Top each cupcake with

½ a Tablespoon of cream cheese and 1 mini oreo. Then add some more batter until the cups are ¾ 's full.
Bake for 19 to 22 minutes or until a toothpick or skewer pole into the middle comes out clean. When cooled, add the whipped topping and cookies left over.

Brownie Cupcakes

Servings: 12

Ingredients:

¾ cup all-purpose flour
1 ½ cups sweetener
3 Tablespoons cocoa
½ teaspoon baking soda
¼ teaspoon table salt
½ cup water
¼ cup unsweetened applesauce
½ teaspoon vinegar
1½ teaspoon margarine, melted
½ teaspoon vanilla extract
Preparation:
Place the oven on to a temperature of 180 Degrees Celsius.

In a bowl, mix together flour, brown sugar, cocoa, baking soda and salt. In another bowl, mix together all of the left over ingredients. Combine both bowls slowly using a wooden spoon. Either use a greased muffin tin or a muffin tin with cupcake holder and fill them up to 3/4's full. Bake for 18 to 20 minutes or until a toothpick or skewer pole into the middle comes out clean.

Marble Cupcakes

Servings: 24

Ingredients:

1 cup flour
½ teaspoon baking powder
¼ teaspoon baking soda
a pinch salt
¾ cup sweeteners
¼ cup canola oil
1 egg
1/3 cup fat free buttermilk
½ crushed pineapple, undrained
½ teaspoon coconut extract

* You can use food colouring to tint the different layers of batter before mixing into the cupcake tray.

Preparation:
Place the oven on to a temperature of 180 Degrees Celsius.
In a bowl, mix together flour, baking powder, baking soda and salt. In another bowl, mix together sugar, oil, coconut extract and egg until smooth. Combine them slowly using a wooden spoon and alternating with the buttermilk. Then add in the pineapple.
Either use a greased muffin tin or a muffin tin with cupcake holder and fill them up to 3/4's full. Bake for 20 to 25 minutes or until a toothpick or skewer pole into the middle comes out clean.

Chocolate Yum Cupcakes

Servings: 24

Ingredients:
1 cup flour
½ cup cocoa
½ teaspoon baking soda
¼ teaspoon salt
2 egg whites
1 whole egg
1 cup sugar

¼ cup canola or vegetable oil
½ cup fat free chocolate milk
2 teaspoons instant espresso coffee granules
1½ teaspoons vanilla

Preparation:
Place the oven on to a temperature of 190 Degrees Celsius.
In a bowl, mix together the flour, cocoa, baking soda and salt. In another bowl, mix together egg whites, whole egg, sugar and oil and beat well. Slowly add the flour mix and the milk until mixed together well. Then add the coffee granules and the vanilla extract.
Either use a greased muffin tin or a muffin tin with cupcake holder and fill them up to 3/4's full. Bake for 15 to 20 minutes or until a toothpick or skewer pole into the middle comes out clean.

Bulk Beer Based Cupcakes

Servings: 288

Ingredients:

34 cups cocoa

4 cups sweetener

1 teaspoon baking soda

1 pinch fine salt

1 bottle Guiness

1 stick melted butter

1 Tablespoon vanilla extract

3 eggs

34 cups sour cream

225g cream cheese

78 cups heavy cream

500g confectioners' sugar

Preparation:

Place the oven on to a temperature of 180 Degrees Celsius.
In a bowl, mix together the flour, cocoa, baking soda and salt. In another bowl, mix together the stout, melted butter, and vanilla. Add the eggs and beat well. Add the sour cream and mix until smooth. Add the dry mix into the wet mix.
Either use a greased muffin tin or a muffin tin with cupcake holder and fill them up to 3/4's full. Bake for about 12 minutes and then rotate the pans. Bake another 12 to 13 minutes until risen, nicely domed, and set in the middle but still soft and tender.

Chocolate Sweet Love Cupcakes

Servings: 12

Ingredients:

1½ cup flour

1 cup sweetener

1 cup water

¼ cups chocolate chips

3 Tablespoons cocoa

½ Tablespoon Salt

1 Tablespoon white vinegar

1 teaspoon baking soda

3 Tablespoons fat free sour cream

1 teaspoon vanilla

3 Tablespoons applesauce

Preparation:

Place the oven on to a temperature of 180 Degrees Celsius. Make four holes in the dry ingredients so that you can pour the vinegar into the first well, then add the sour cream into the second well. Pour the vanilla into the third well and in the fourth well, pour the applesauce. Pour the water over the wells and then mix together with a whisk until smooth. Add the chocolate chips.

Either use a greased muffin tin or a muffin tin with cupcake holder and fill them up to 3/4's full. Bake for 20 to 25 minutes or until a toothpick or skewer pole into the middle comes out clean.

Sinless Chocolate Fun

Servings: 12

Ingredients:

3/4 cup purpose flour
¼ cup cocoa powder
¼ teaspoon salt
½ teaspoon baking powder
3/4 teaspoon baking soda
9 Tablespoons pure maple syrup
20 drops stevia extract
6 Tablespoons eggs
2 tsp vanilla extract

Preparation:
Place the oven on to a temperature of 180 Degrees Celsius.
In a bowl, mix together the dry ingredients. In another bowl, mix together the wet ingredients. Slowly add the two together until mixed together well.
Either use a greased muffin tin or a muffin tin with cupcake holder and fill them up to 3/4's full. Bake for 25 minutes or until a toothpick or skewer pole into the middle comes out clean.

Strawberry Vanilla Fun Cupcakes

Servings: 12

Ingredients:

1 cup self-rising flour

½ cup fat free milk powder

1 box Jello Cook and Serve Strawberry Pudding Mix

½ cup sweetener

1 teaspoon vanilla

120g unsweetened applesauce

¼ teaspoon baking soda

4 egg whites

1 pinch of salt

Preparation:

Place the oven on to a temperature of 180 Degrees Celsius.
Mix together the flour, milk powder, Jello mix, cocoa, and sweetener in a bowl. In another bowl, mix together the vanilla, applesauce and the baking soda. IN another bowl beat the egg whites until they form peaks. Fold in the applesauce mix and beat together for about two minutes.
Either use a greased muffin tin or a muffin tin with cupcake holder and fill them up to 3/4's full. Bake for 18 - 20 minutes or until a toothpick or skewer pole into the middle comes out clean.

CPSIA information can be obtained
at www.ICGtesting.com
Printed in the USA
BVHW050326070223
658034BV00030B/500